STUDY GUIDE TO

# THE THEORY OF MONEY AND CREDIT

*Study Guide*

TO

# THE THEORY OF MONEY AND CREDIT

LUDWIG VON MISES

*Robert P. Murphy*

LvMI

MISES INSTITUTE

*The Theory of Money and Credit* was translated from the German by H.E. Batson and published by Jonathan Cape (London) in 1934.



Ludwig von Mises Institute
518 West Magnolia Avenue
Auburn, Alabama 36832
Mises.org

ISBN: 978-1-61016-235-7

# CONTENTS

## III. MONEY AND BANKING



## IV. MONETARY RECONSTRUCTION

## APPENDICES

# PREFACE

When "Joe the Plumber"—a small business owner who became a hero among conservatives when he challenged candidate Barack Obama's proposed tax hikes in the 2008 presidential campaign—compiled a list of Christmas book recommendations for *The American Spectator*, he included *The Theory of Money and Credit*, saying it was "important reading for these troubled times." Although Austrians were glad that someone was bringing attention to Mises's classic work, many were understandably skeptical. After all, *The Theory of Money and Credit* is a *hard* book to read.

The present study guide seeks to change that common impression. In preparing it, I have found that Mises's work can be difficult at times, but there is a definite *method* behind it. In other words, if the reader will put in the effort to work through the book methodically, he or she will see that Mises systematically builds his argument from one chapter to the next. With the help of this study guide, even the layperson will be able to unlock the amazing insights contained in this tome, first published a century ago.

One of the most enjoyable surprises for me was to discover just how impressive an economist Ludwig von Mises really was, even at a relatively young age. In this single work, Mises integrated (what we now call) microeconomics with macroeconomics. He successfully applied subjectivist, marginal utility theory to the case of money—a task that had eluded earlier theorists in the Austrian tradition. As if that weren't enough, Mises gave a systematic explanation of the boom-bust cycle, blaming it on the artificial expansion of bank credit and the corresponding reduction of the money rate of interest below the "natural" rate.

These accomplishments alone would have earned Mises an important seat in the history of economic thought. Yet upon my most recent reading, I realized that Mises showcases much more of his talent. For one thing, he displays a thorough command of the relevant literature, not only in pure economic theory but also in applied topics such as money and banking. He also shows a practical understanding of actual financial markets, which often behave differently from the depiction in academic writings. In the final section of the book (written after the original release), Mises offers very wise policy recommendations for returning to sound money.

The format of the study guide follows the 1953 edition of *The Theory of Money and Credit* published by the Mises Institute. I follow Mises's work very closely, down to the individual section headings. Each chapter contains an overall summary (except for very short chapters), followed by a detailed outline. Then I include a section on either "Notable Contributions" or "Technical Notes." There is also a list of new terms for each chapter (with a full list included in the back as a glossary) and finally a list of five study questions to ensure that the reader is grasping the essential points of each chapter.

In order to modernize the style, hyphens have been dropped, and in a few instances, spelling has been updated. However, no content has been altered from the English translation as published by the Mises Institute.

I hope that this study guide eases the understandable "intimidation factor" and allows a new generation of readers to experience the wealth of wisdom contained in Mises's first major work. As an insightful plumber (and layperson) has remarked, it is important reading for these troubled times.

Robert P. Murphy<br>Nashville, Tennessee<br>July, 2011

PART I

# THE NATURE OF MONEY

CHAPTER I

# THE FUNCTION OF MONEY

## *Summary*

Money is necessary in a society based on private property and the division of labor. The function of money is to facilitate these trades: Money is a commonly used medium of exchange.

In a **direct exchange**, people accept goods in trade that they intend to personally use, whether for consumption or production. There is no medium of exchange involved in the transaction.

In an **indirect exchange**, at least one person in the transaction accepts a good that he intends to trade away in the future for something else. The item that is accepted in the first trade is a medium of exchange.

Even before the use of money, traders would have quickly discovered the benefits of indirect exchanges, and the use of media of exchange to facilitate them. Some goods would have had a far broader market than others. A trader who came to market with an unmarketable good would place himself in a more advantageous bargaining position if he engaged in an indirect exchange, by trading his good for something that was more marketable.

Because every trader would act in this fashion, those goods that were initially more marketable, would see their marketability enhanced even further. Over time, a community would gravitate to one or a few commodities that would be acceptable to everyone in trade. This is how money emerged from an initial state of barter. Historically the market has often chosen gold and silver as money.

Although other writers outline other "functions" of money—such as a standard of deferred payments or a store of value—these all flow from its definition: money is a commonly accepted medium of exchange.

## *Chapter Outline*

### 1. The General Economic Conditions for the Use of Money

A person living by himself on a tropical island would not need **money**. Several people living in the same household would not need money either, so long as they produced everything they needed within the household. Even an entire community—consisting of thousands or millions of households, each of which specialized in producing different goods and services—could get by without the use of money, assuming there were a central group or person who acted as a "planner" and told everyone what to make, and decided which portion of the total output each person would get to consume.

However, in a society based on the **division of labor**, and where private individuals own both consumption goods (TVs, radios, Big Macs) and producer goods (tractors, factories, copper mines), money is essential. In such a society, there is no one person or group who decides how scarce resources will be deployed. Each individual must make his or her own plans, which usually require exchanging property for other people's property. The function of money is to facilitate these trades: Money is a commonly used **medium of exchange**.

### 2. The Origin of Money

In a **direct exchange**, people accept goods in trade that they intend to personally use, whether for consumption or production. For example, suppose Alan has a muffin but he is really hungry for fish. Bill, on the other hand, has a net (which can be used to catch fish) that he doesn't really want, but he thinks Alan's muffin looks delicious. If Alan trades his muffin for Bill's net, this is a direct exchange. There is no medium of exchange involved in the transaction.

In an **indirect exchange**, at least one person in the transaction accepts a good that he *doesn't* intend to consume or use himself in production. Rather, the person accepts a good because he plans on trading it away again in the future. For example, suppose there is a woman who has knitted a quilt, and she wants to exchange it for a certain parakeet. Unfortunately, the man who owns the parakeet doesn't want a quilt, but is instead interested in obtaining a new radio. The owner of the radio, however, hates birds, but is very cold at night. The woman with the quilt, unfortunately, is very hard of hearing and has no use for a radio.

In this scenario, no direct exchange is possible. However, the woman could trade away her quilt for the radio—even though she personally has no use for it—and then trade the radio in turn for the parakeet. These two successive trades would make all three people happier. In this example, the radio would be a medium of exchange.

Logically, there must have been a time when people had goods and traded with each other, but before money had arisen. Even before the use of money, traders would have quickly discovered the benefits of indirect exchanges—and the use of media of exchange to facilitate them.

Some goods (eggs, milk, leather) would have had a far broader market than others (telescopes, philosophy books, machinery). A trader who came to market with an unmarketable good such as a telescope probably wouldn't be able to quickly find someone who (*a*) had the items that the first trader hoped to acquire and (*b*) wanted a telescope. In this case, the trader could improve his bargaining position by trading away his telescope for something more marketable, such as eggs, even if the trader had no desire to eat the eggs.

Because every trader would act in this fashion, those goods that were initially more marketable, would see their marketability enhanced even further: They would be demanded not only by people intending to use them directly, but also by people intending to use them as media of exchange. In any particular indirect exchange, a trader would naturally prefer to sell his own wares in exchange for the most marketable medium of exchange, because this would place him in the most advantageous position as he continued looking for the goods he ultimately desired. Over time, a community would gravitate to one or a few commodities that would be acceptable to everyone in trade. A commonly accepted medium of exchange *is* money.

Historically, gold and silver have been the two commodities most frequently employed as money. They have very similar properties and are both excellent media of exchange.

## 3. The "Secondary" Functions of Money

Money is, by definition, a common medium of exchange, which therefore serves to facilitate the exchange of goods and services. In a market economy, this is a crucial "function" and we see money's importance by focusing on it. Although other writers outline other "functions" of money—such as a standard of deferred payments, or a facilitator of credit transactions, or a store of value through time—these all flow from its use as a common medium of exchange.

## *Important Contributions*

- Mises references Carl Menger, whose 1871 *Grundsätze* (translated as *Principles of Economics*) is the founding work of what is called "Austrian" economics. Among his other contributions, Menger is credited in the annals of the history of economic thought with giving the first satisfactory explanation of the origin of money. Rather than assuming that money must have been created by an edict issued by a powerful king or wise tribal leader, Menger showed that step-by-step evolution from an initial state of barter to a monetary economy, where each person only seeks to improve his own position at each step in the process.

- Even in modern textbooks, writers will list several "functions" of money. This can be confusing, because it makes it hard to pin down exactly what money *is* and why it so important. Menger's approach —followed by Mises—is refreshingly clear: Money is defined as a commonly accepted medium of exchange, and this characteristic enables all of the other "functions" attributed to it.

## *New Terminology*

**Direct exchange:** An exchange in which both parties intend to directly use the received good, either in consumption or production.

**Indirect exchange:** An exchange in which at least one party intends to hold the received good, in order to trade it away in the future for something else.

**Division of labor:** The situation in which people specialize in particular occupations, producing far more than they personally can consume, and trade away their surplus to receive some of the surplus created by others.

**Medium of exchange:** A good that is accepted in exchange, with the intention of trading it away to acquire something else in the future.

**Money:** A medium of exchange that is generally accepted in the community. Money typically stands on one side of virtually every exchange.

## *Study Questions*

1. Would a society based on total central planning in both production and consumption need money? Why or why not? (p. 29)

2. Why doesn't a direct exchange involve the use of a medium of exchange? (p. 30)

3. Can you think of reasons that traders eventually gravitated toward gold and silver as money, as opposed to other items such as cattle or aluminum?

4. Did media of exchange exist *before* the existence of money? (pp. 30–32)

5. For the various secondary functions of money listed by Mises, explain how each is related to money's role as a commonly accepted medium of exchange. (pp. 34–36)

CHAPTER 2

# ON THE MEASUREMENT OF VALUE

## *Summary*


The classical economists relied on an **objective theory of value**, and naturally thought that money was a measuring rod of this objective value. Modern economics is based on a **subjective theory of value**, which traces the source of value to the mind of the individual actor. **Value** is the significance given to a particular good by a person.

Subjective value is bound up with the idea of exchange. Each party to a voluntary trade gives up an item that is lower on his value ranking (or **scale of values**), in exchange for an item that is higher on his ranking. Exchanges will occur until there are no more mutually beneficial trades. Individuals' subjective valuations give rise to *objective* exchange ratios or **prices**.

The **law of diminishing marginal utility** states that the value of the last unit of a commodity decreases as the person acquires a greater quantity of the commodity. The various schemes to define an objective measurement of satisfaction—a "util"—cannot get around the fact that value scales involve a ranking (1st, 2nd, 3rd, etc.) and not a measurement of the intensity of value. It is impossible to perform arithmetical operations on the marginal utilities of various units in order to compute the "total utility" or total value of the entire stock of the good. If someone says, "Diamonds are more valuable than water," what he means is that if forced to give up *one* diamond or *one* gallon of water, he would choose to give up the latter.

Knowledge of objective money prices causes people to revise their subjective value scales. Objective money prices provide a "common denominator" for the market exchange values of all the various goods and services available.

However, money prices themselves are constantly changing. That is why Mises and Menger prefer to say that money is an index (not a measurement) of prices, since it is less liable to confusion.

## *Chapter Outline*

### 1. The Immeasurability of Subjective Use-Values

The classical economists (such as Adam Smith) relied on an **objective theory of value**, which held that the value of a commodity was based on an objective criterion (such as the amount of labor required for its production). In this mindset, it was natural to view money as a measuring rod of this objective value. Just as a thermometer shows a higher reading on a hot day than on a cold day—reflecting the objectively warmer temperature—so too did the classical economists think that a higher price tag indicated that a more expensive good had a higher objective value than a cheaper good.

However, modern economics is based on a **subjective theory of value**, which traces the source of value to the mind of the individual actor. In modern economics, value doesn't reside in physical things per se, but instead is an attribute ascribed to physical things by subjective preferences. **Value** is the significance given to a particular good by a person, who can imagine ways to use the good to become more satisfied.

Subjective value is bound up with the idea of exchange. If a man values a piece of iron more than a piece of bread, it means that he would choose the former if faced with a choice between the two. Even Robinson Crusoe, alone on his desert island, reveals his valuations by his "exchanges" with nature. For example, he may value satisfying his hunger more than he values satisfying his desire to lounge on the beach, and that is why he "exchanges" his leisure time for coconuts (by climbing trees).

With more than one person, valuation guides exchanges made in the marketplace. Each party to a voluntary trade gives up an item that is lower on his value ranking (or **scale of values**), in exchange for an item that is higher on his ranking. This apparent contradiction—where each person gives up something "less valuable" in exchange for something "more valuable"—is perfectly sensible because value is in the eye of the beholder, i.e., value is subjective.

In the market, exchanges will occur until there are no more mutually beneficial trades. The underlying subjective valuations *driving* acts of exchange do not involve a "measurement" of value. (For an analogy, someone can rank his friends in order of importance, without implying that there is an objective unit of friendship that the person measures in each person before constructing the ranking. Someone can report, "Jim is my best friend and Sally is my second-best friend" without being able to say, "Jim is a 24 percent better friend than Sally.") All that is necessary is that a person be able to look at any two possibilities, and decide which he prefers.

Even though market exchanges are driven by subjective valuations that are themselves nonquantifiable, nonetheless these exchanges in turn give rise to *objective* exchange ratios or **prices**. For example, suppose Alice has three pears while Bob has two apples, and that on her value scale Alice ranks "two apples" more highly than "three pears," whereas Bob has the opposite ranking. These subjective valuations—which do not involve any measurement of the amount of value or utility residing in each combination of fruit—mean that the two people can gain from trading the three pears for the two apples. This mutually beneficial trade then establishes that the objective price of an apple is 1.5 pears, and that the price of a pear is two-thirds of an apple. Thus Alice and Bob's subjective rankings of apples and pears, allowed for the formation of an objective market price reflected in their exchange. But it would be nonsensical to describe this scenario as one in which "an apple gives 50 percent more value to people than a pear."

The **law of diminishing marginal utility** states that the value of the last unit of a commodity (in someone's possession) decreases as the person acquires a greater quantity of the commodity. This follows from the observation that a person will necessarily assign subsequent units of a commodity to those purposes that he deems less and less significant. For example, if a person has only one gallon of water, he will attach a great significance to it, because it is necessary to stave off thirst.

As a person's access to water becomes greater, however, the last (or marginal) gallon of water becomes less significant. The 25th gallon, perhaps, will be devoted to cooking, and is not nearly as important as the 1st through 24th gallons, which were devoted to drinking. And the 1,000th gallon might be used to wash the car, a relatively unimportant goal.

The various schemes to define an objective measurement of satisfaction—a "util"—cannot get around the fact that value scales involve a ranking (1st, 2nd, 3rd, etc.) and not a measurement of the intensity of value. The renowned Chicago School economist Irving Fisher, for example, devised a clever argument by which he equated the utility of the 100th loaf of bread with the utility derived from the last and second-last units of fuel oil. At the same time, the utility of the 150th loaf of bread was equal to the utility of only the last unit of fuel oil. Fisher concludes that the 150th loaf of bread must have only one-half the utility of the 100th loaf. But this assumes away diminishing marginal utility in the fuel oil.

## 2. Total Value

If it is impossible to measure the value in a single unit of a good, it is obviously impossible to perform arithmetical operations on the marginal utilities of various units in order to compute the "total utility" or total value of the entire stock of the good. One problem with this approach is that a **free good** (such as air) would end up with a total value of zero, since the marginal utility of one cubic meter of air is zero in most circumstances.

It must be repeated that utility or value is a concept related to the acts of choice that a particular individual contemplates. If someone says, "Diamonds are more valuable than water," what he means is that if forced to give up *one* diamond or *one* gallon of water, he would choose to give up the latter. But if an individual had to choose between all the water in the world, or all the diamonds, then he would choose to retain the water (at least if he wanted to live longer than a few days). Only in this contrived case can we meaningfully speak of the "total value" of the entire stock of water, because in this situation the "total value" and the "marginal value" are the same; the unit under consideration is all the water in the world.

## 3. Money as a Price Index

At this point, it should be clear that money cannot serve as a measuring rod of subjective value. There is a sense in which money is a measure of objective market exchange value, however. For example, if a car trades for $20,000 while a motorcycle trades for $10,000, then the car has twice as much exchange value. Someone bringing a car to market can obtain "twice as many goods and services" for it, where the amount is measured in money prices.

Knowledge of objective money prices causes people to revise their subjective value scales. Someone who despises smoking and loves vegetables may nonetheless place a higher value on an unopened carton of cigarettes than on a tomato, because she can sell the carton for money, and then use the money to buy a tomato as well as many other items. In this way, objective money prices provide a "common denominator" for the market exchange values of all the various goods and services available.

However, because money prices themselves are determined by the underlying subjective valuations of the traders, they are constantly changing. The various combinations of goods that one motorcycle can "buy" today, may be different tomorrow, not only because the price (quoted in money) of the motorcycle can change, but also because the prices (quoted in money) of all others goods can change. That is why Mises and Menger prefer to say that money is an index (not a measurement) of prices, since it is less liable to confusion.

## *Important Contributions*

- The replacement of the classical economists' labor (or cost) theory of value, with subjective value theory, was a true revolution in economic theory. The classical theory explained the price of a good by the amount of labor or (more generally) the cost of producing the good. Although such an approach explained the fact that prices and production costs tended to be similar, there were many problems. For example, it was clear that the *actual* day-to-day prices of goods were not determined by production costs, so at best the cost theory explained long-run tendencies, not the determinants of actual market prices. Worse still, "costs" are themselves prices, and so to explain the price of a good by the costs of producing it, only pushes the problem back one step. By explaining the prices of consumer goods through the interaction of subjective valuations in the market—and then using these consumer prices to explain the prices of the producer goods needed to make them—the subjective value theorists resolved these problems. Although other economists participated in the Subjectivist/Marginal Revolution, it was the Austrian economists who worked out the logical foundations of the new approach, as Mises's frequent references to Menger, Böhm-Bawerk, and Wieser testify.

- Irving Fisher was an incredibly influential economist from the Chicago School, and arguably one of the founders of modern, mainstream economics. Although economists paid lip service to the subjectivist revolution in value theory, nonetheless they often fell back into the old habit of viewing utility as a cardinal, measurable substance. Mises's critique of Fisher is a good illustration of this tendency. Modern Austrian economists also chide their mainstream peers for relying on mathematical models of "utility functions" that can easily lead the economist into forgetting that modern price theory only assumes that individuals can *rank* various combinations of goods from best to worst. There is no need to assume that a consumer has an intensity of preference for various goods that could be measured by units of utility.

## *New Terminology*

**Free good:** A good that has a price of zero, because it is not scarce. There is enough of the good to satisfy all human wants that it can technically fulfill.

**Law of diminishing marginal utility:** The rule, deducible from the nature of economizing action, that each additional unit of a good or service will have a lower value, because a person will allocate successive units to satisfying ends that are less and less important.

**Objective theory of value:** An explanation of value that relies on the objective properties of a good, such as its cost of production or the amount of labor that went into its construction. (The classical economists, such as Adam Smith and David Ricardo, held an objective theory of value.)

**Prices:** The market exchange ratios between various goods and services. In a monetary economy, prices are typically quoted in terms of the money good.

**Scale of values:** An analytical tool by which the economist interprets the actions of an individual, who subjectively ranks particular units of goods and services in order from most to least important.

**Subjective theory of value:** An explanation of value that relies on individuals' subjective rankings of particular units of goods and services. (The so-called Marginal Revolution of the early 1870s—spearheaded by Carl Menger, William Stanley Jevons, and Léon Walras—overturned the objective theory of value and ushered in the subjective theory.)

**Value:** The importance that an individual places on a particular unit of a good or service.

## Study Questions

1. Explain: "In the older political economy, the search for a principle governing the measurement of value was to a certain extent justifiable." (p. 38)

2. Why would an isolated individual still need to engage in a "comparison of values" before taking action with respect to scarce goods? (p. 38)

3. Why does an exchange of two items require that the people making the exchange place the items in reverse order on their value scales? (p. 39)

4. Explain: "The untenability of [Wieser's] argument is shown by the fact that it would prove that the total stock of a free good must always be worth nothing." (p. 45)

5. How does money aid the entrepreneur? (pp. 48–49)

CHAPTER 3

# THE VARIOUS KINDS OF MONEY

## *Summary*

A **money substitute** is a perfectly secure and immediate claim on money. Because the claims themselves can facilitate indirect exchange, they become a "substitute" for the original commodity money.

The definition of *money* should serve the purposes of economic theory, the most important being the explanation of the **purchasing power** of money. For economics, what matters is the actual practices and expectations of individuals in the market, rather than legal formalities.

**Commodity money** is a common medium of exchange that is also an economic good in its own right. For example, gold, silver, and even tobacco have historically been used as money, and yet people also valued and traded these commodities for other reasons.

**Fiat money** is accepted as a common medium of exchange *not* because of its technological properties, but because of a special legal designation provided by the appropriate authority. For example, in the current United States "green rectangular pieces of paper" become money when certain ink patterns are placed on them.

**Credit money** occurs when a claim on a physical or legal person, falling due in the future, is itself used as a medium of exchange.

Some theorists explain the value of money as due to State commands. But the government cannot force people to adopt a particular item as the commonly accepted medium of exchange, let alone to accept it with a particular purchasing power. The government can use its tremendous power to make it more likely that people will adopt a particular item (such as green pieces of paper with certain ink patterns) as money, but economically something is money because of its usage by people in the market. A government edict per se cannot transform it into money.

## *Chapter Outline*

### 1. Money and Money Substitutes

A **money substitute** is a perfectly secure and immediate claim on money. For example, suppose the commonly accepted medium of exchange is gold, and a reputable bank issues a paper ticket entitling the bearer to one ounce of gold. So long as people in the community are certain that they will be paid in physical gold whenever they present the ticket to a branch of the bank, then such tickets are money substitutes and may change hands during purchases the same way physical gold would.

In the market economy, people can issue perfectly secure and immediate claims (i.e., redemption tickets) to all sorts of goods, not just money. But the crucial feature of such claims on money is that the claims themselves can facilitate indirect exchange, and so become a "substitute" for the original commodity money. In other words, pieces of paper entitling the owner to an ounce of gold can circulate in the market the same way actual 1 oz. gold coins would (so long as everyone is assured of immediate redemption). In principle merchants might never actually turn the tickets in, to receive the physical gold. In contrast, people might trade paper claims guaranteeing the owner to a loaf of bread, but they would eventually redeem them. Such tickets could never become "bread-substitutes" because the paper couldn't serve the same function as actual bread.

For economists—as opposed to legal theorists or the business-person—the definition of *money* should serve the purposes of economic theory. The central task of the economic analysis of money is to explain the exchange ratios between money and all other goods, i.e., to explain the **purchasing power** of money.

In Mises's judgment, the most fruitful classification scheme distinguishes between the underlying "**money in the narrower sense**" versus perfectly secure and immediate *claims* to such money, i.e., money substitutes. He concedes that it would be logically consistent to include money substitutes in the definition of *money* itself, but believes his preferred distinction (i.e., between money and money substitutes) will make it easier to explain other phenomena (such as the purchasing power of money, as well as the boom-bust cycle) more clearly in later chapters. (See the Appendix B on page 231 for a diagram outlining Mises's classification scheme for various items that are often included in the concept of money.)

## 2. The Peculiarities of Money Substitutes

In the economic analysis of money, what matters is the actual practices and expectations of individuals in the market. For example, whether or not legislation declares that **token coins** are *legally binding* claims on money, if *in practice* the holder of a token can easily exchange it for the "equivalent" amount of actual money, then *economically speaking* the token is a money substitute.

The same principle applies to **banknotes**. For example, conventional accounts say that Austria-Hungary from 1900 to 1914 possessed a **paper standard**, because *legally* the Austro-Hungarian Bank had no obligation to redeem its paper notes for commodity money, and in fact the notes were declared **legal tender**. Yet in practice during this period, the Austro-Hungarian Bank would voluntarily **cash** its paper notes for gold upon request, and so economically speaking Austria-Hungary was on a **gold standard**.

## 3. Commodity Money, Credit Money, and Fiat Money

**Commodity money** is a common medium of exchange that is also an economic good in its own right. For example, gold, silver, and even tobacco have historically been used as money, and yet people also valued and traded these commodities for other reasons.

**Fiat money** is accepted as a common medium of exchange *not* because of its technological properties, but because of a special legal designation provided by the appropriate authority. For example, in the current United States "green rectangular pieces of paper" are not money per se. They only become money when they are cut to exact size and printed with the correct designs by the U.S. Treasury. Thus the green pieces of paper appear to become money by "fiat" (i.e., command) of the U.S. government. However, in economics the definition of money is a commonly accepted medium of exchange. The government can only use its powers to encourage people to use a particular class of items—for example, green pieces of paper with the appropriate ink patterns—as a common medium of exchange; the mere legal declaration isn't what makes them money, economically speaking.

**Credit money** occurs when a claim on a physical or legal person (e.g., a corporation or government agency), falling due in the future, is itself used as a medium of exchange. To distinguish credit *money* from mere credit, it is necessary that people are generally willing to accept the claim in trade *not* because they want to wait and receive the underlying payment (to which the claim entitles them), but because they expect to be able to easily trade away the claim itself for other goods. For example, suppose a government originally promised to redeem its paper notes immediately upon demand for commodity money (such as gold). But during a war, the government suspends convertibility, so that the paper notes are now not legally binding claims on anything. However, if the public expects that at some point in the future, redeemability will be restored, then the notes would circulate as credit money (not fiat money) because they would be claims to gold falling due in the future (at an uncertain date). So long as the paper notes are considered so **liquid** that virtually everyone is willing to accept them in trade, they are a common medium of exchange and hence money.

## 4. The Commodity Money of the Past and of the Present

Some theorists explain the value of money as due to State commands. For example, "The monetary unit of the United States is the dollar, because the U.S. government has passed a law." But this is a very inadequate reading of history, because governments cannot simply force a particular good to command a particular *purchasing power* in the market. For example, a king can collect taxes in the form of silver coins, and then **debase** them by melting them down and minting a greater number of coins with less silver content per coin. But the market will react by raising prices (quoted in terms of the coins), and even if the king resorts to **price controls** with draconian penalties, he will cause shortages in accordance with economic law.

## *Technical Notes*

- On pages 56–57, Mises argues that token coinage is not an independent economic concept, but rather a special type of money substitute. Token coinage was developed to facilitate small transactions. For example, in a country using gold as its commodity money, it would be awkward to purchase an item with a price of $\frac{1}{100}$th of an ounce of gold, if customers had to use the physical gold itself. The government might therefore produce a limited number of small discs (perhaps made of copper or nickel) that were stamped with, "Legal Tender, $\frac{1}{100}$th oz. of gold." Even though the actual metal content of the tokens would be less, they would nonetheless trade at their face value so long as everyone believed that the government would faithfully exchange one ounce of physical gold for 100 tokens. The important point is not whether such redemption were a legal requirement, but merely whether *in practice* people expected the option to be available upon demand. (Also note that the "coins" Mises discusses on pages 50–51 are *not* token coins, but coins consisting of the commodity money. In other words, such coins are valued because they actually *consist of* a recognized weight in gold or silver, not because the holders expect to be able to *redeem* them for gold or silver.)

- In the Misesian scheme, credit money is not the same as a money substitute because the claims constituting credit money are not due immediately, whereas they must be for a true money substitute. Money substitutes are valued the same as the underlying money to which they are claims; a banknote entitling the bearer to one ounce of gold, upon request, will have the same purchasing power as one ounce of gold. However, a corporate bond promising the bearer one ounce of gold in 30 years, if it is to become a credit money and circulate as a common medium of exchange, will be subject to an independent valuation, depending not merely on the reliability of the claim and the wait involved, but also on the liquidity of the bond. (See p. 61.)

## *New Terminology*

**Banknotes:** Paper notes issued by banks, typically entitling the bearer to a specified amount of the money good.

**Cash (verb):** To redeem a claim (such as a banknote) by paying the specified amount of the money good.

**Commodity money:** A common medium of exchange that is an economic good in its own right, valued for nonmonetary reasons.

**Credit money:** A common medium of exchange that is a claim on a person or legal person (such as a corporation or government agency), not falling due until a (possibly uncertain) future date.

**Debase:** To dilute the value of the money, for example when a ruler introduces "base" metals into the coinage, reducing their precious-metal content.

**Fiat money:** A common medium of exchange accepted not because of its technological properties, but because of a special legal designation provided by the appropriate authority. Fiat money is not "backed up" by anything else.

**Gold standard:** The arrangement by which a nation's money (such as the U.S. dollar or the British pound) can be redeemed for a definite weight of gold.

**Legal tender:** An item that the government declares to be valid for the payment of debts denominated in money, at par value.

**Liquid (adjective):** The ability of being sold for the full market price with a very short search time. (For example, a share of corporate stock is much more liquid than a house.)

**Money in the narrower sense:** The actual money good (whether commodity, fiat, or credit money), not including money substitutes.

**Money in the broader sense:** The actual money good (whether commodity, fiat, or credit money), plus money substitutes.

**Money substitute:** A perfectly secure and instantly redeemable claim on money, which itself circulates as money (in the broader sense) because it fulfills the functions of money.

**Paper standard:** The arrangement by which the government does not redeem paper notes for a precious metal. (A paper standard stands in contrast to a gold standard.)

**Price controls:** Government decrees threatening fines or other punishment for people trading at prices that are either too high (in the case of a price ceiling) or too low (in the case of a price floor).

**Purchasing power:** The amount of goods and services that a unit of money can command because of the various prices in the market.

**Token coins:** Coins that serve as representatives of money (usually in very small denominations), even though they do not contain the full weight of metal in the case of a commodity money.

## *Study Questions*

1. What is "peculiar" about the fact that people may use claims on money, rather than money itself? How is this peculiarity "explained by reference to the special characteristics of money"? (p. 50)

2. What does Mises think of the treatment economists had given to money, before his own contribution? (p. 51)

3. What is the task of economic theory, regarding money? (p. 51)

4. Explain: "[W]hereas it is impossible to satisfy an increase in the demand, say, for bread by issuing more bread-tickets ... it is perfectly possible to satisfy an increased demand for money by just such a process as this." (p. 53)

5. Would Mises be surprised at the world's current monetary system? (p. 61)

CHAPTER 4

# MONEY AND THE STATE

## *Summary*

Unless it resorts to outright socialism, the State must conform to the market. Its actions in the market are governed by the Laws of Price. In this respect, the State has more influence than any other entity, but this is due to the State's enormous budget.

In economics, money is a common medium of exchange. But from the legal point of view, money is a common medium of payment or debt settlement. Money can only serve this function (as a medium of debt settlement) because it is a medium of exchange. This is clear when we consider cases where a contract cannot be fulfilled as written, and so the court specifies a monetary payment instead.

Government cannot force people to attribute a certain exchange value to a good. The legal system can certainly allow debtors to "satisfy" their contractual liabilities by paying with items at a face value higher than what the creditors actually believe they are worth, but this merely means a partial repudiation of the debt.

Originally the State's only role in the monetary sphere was to supply recognizable coins that were hard to counterfeit and that were very similar in appearance, weight, and fineness. By producing suitable coins, the State was merely facilitating commerce, because merchants wouldn't need chemical tests and scales to evaluate the gold or silver their customers presented in payment.

The State's influence in the monetary sphere has grown because its size has grown, but also because of its control of the mint: The State can withdraw coins of one metal and replace them with coins of a different metal. The State also influences the monetary sphere through its ability to suspend the immediate redemption of money substitutes, converting them into credit money or even fiat money.

## *Chapter Outline*

### 1. The Position of the State in the Market

Although it commands a large influence because of its power to tax, ultimately the State must conform to the market. Unless it completely abolishes private property and forms a socialist State, the government can only successfully change market prices through its own decisions to buy and sell. The same is true of money: mere government edicts cannot explain the purchasing power of a common medium of exchange.

### 2. The Legal Concept of Money

In economics, money is a common medium of exchange. But from the legal point of view, money is a common medium of payment or debt settlement. If a contract calls for one party to pay back a loan of "100 ounces of gold, plus 5 ounces in interest" in one year, the legal system must specify what types of goods are acceptable to satisfy the contract. (For example, must it be done in physical gold, or can a banknote or a check written on a bank account—denominated in gold—satisfy the debt? What about token coins that can be exchanged for gold?) However, money can only serve this function (as a medium of debt settlement) because it is a medium of exchange. This is clear when we consider cases where a contract cannot be fulfilled as written, and so the court specifies a monetary payment instead.

Government cannot force people to attribute a certain exchange value to a good. The legal system can certainly allow debtors to "satisfy" their contractual liabilities by paying with items at a face value higher than what the creditors actually believe they are worth, but this merely means a partial repudiation of the debt.

## 3. The Influence of the State on the Monetary System

Originally the State's only role in the monetary sphere was to supply coins of the greatest possible degree of similarity in appearance, weight, and fineness. Furthermore, to do its task well the State would manufacture coins that were hard to counterfeit, and that bore a recognizable stamp. In this regard, the State wasn't *defining* money, but was instead merely taking what *the market* had chosen as the money—for example, gold—and then producing hunks of the money in convenient shapes. By producing suitable coins, the State was merely facilitating commerce: if everyone recognized the State's one-ounce gold coin, and knew that it was genuine, then merchants wouldn't have to resort to chemical tests and scales to evaluate the yellow metal their customers presented in payment.

The State's influence in the monetary sphere has grown because its size (relative to the economy) has grown, but also because of its control of the mint. The State can exert great power over what its subjects choose as the common medium of exchange, since it can (for example) withdraw coins of one metal and replace them with coins of a different metal. Even so, the State cannot avoid the laws of economics. The failed attempts at **bimetallist legislation**—where the government established a fixed ratio between the value of gold and silver—showed the operation of **Gresham's Law**. That is, when the actual market values of gold and silver deviated from the legal ratio, people would hoard the undervalued metal and try to spend the overvalued metal.

The State also influences the monetary sphere through its ability to suspend the immediate redemption of money substitutes, converting them into credit money or even fiat money.

## *Important Contributions*

- Carl Menger's explanation of the origin of money (laid out in chapter 1) offers a satisfactory rebuttal to the "State theory of money" offered by Knapp and other theorists. (p. 73) If an Austrian economist disputes the theory that money derives its value from the State, the argument is more compelling if the Austrian can show—using Menger's approach—how money arose spontaneously on the market.

- In this chapter we already see the benefit of Mises's fastidious classification scheme regarding money. Armed with his categories of money substitutes, commodity money, and credit money, Mises can explain exactly *how* a State influences the money used by its subjects. While many others place great importance on State legislation regarding tax payments and debt contracts, Mises instead looks at the State's role in minting coins and its power to change money substitutes into credit money (by suspending immediate redemption of the claims to money). (pp. 77–78)

## *New Terminology*

**Bimetallist legislation:** Efforts by the government to establish a fixed conversion ratio between gold and silver. For example, the government might require that merchants who post a price in gold ounces, also accept payment in silver ounces at a fixed multiple of the gold price.

**Gresham's Law:** Popularly summarized as "bad money drives out good," the phenomenon by which people will hold money that is undervalued by legislation, and will spend the money that is overvalued by legislation. For example, if bimetallist legislation requires that merchants accept silver and gold at the ratio of 16-to-1, when in fact the actual market exchange rate is 20-to-1, then everyone will try to buy with silver, and no one will use gold for making purchases. Gold will seem to disappear, and only silver will be used in commerce. For a different example, if the government passes legal tender laws on all government-stamped coins, then coins with low metal value (such as U.S. quarters minted in the year 2000) will circulate in trade, whereas coins with high metal content (such as U.S. quarters minted in the year 1950) will be hoarded by people who recognize the value of the silver.

## *Study Questions*

1. Explain: "When notes that are appraised commercially at only half their face-value are proclaimed legal tender, this amounts fundamentally to the same thing as granting debtors legal relief from half of their liabilities." (p. 71)

2. Explain: "State declarations of legal tender affect only those monetary obligations that have already been contracted." (p. 71)

3. What are the two mechanisms through which the "State's influence on commercial usage, both potential and actual, has increased"? (pp. 72–73)

4. Explain: "A country that wishes to persuade its subjects to go over from one precious-metal standard to another cannot rest content with expressing this aspiration in appropriate provisions of the civil and fiscal law." (p. 74)

5. Explain: "The parallel standard was thus turned, not into a double standard, as the legislators had intended, but into an alternative standard." (p. 75)

CHAPTER 5

# MONEY AS AN ECONOMIC GOOD

## *Chapter Outline*

### 1. Money Neither a Production Good nor a Consumption Good

Traditionally, economic goods were divided into consumption goods (what Menger called goods of the first order) and production goods (what Menger called goods of higher orders). Consumption goods directly satisfied human desires, whereas production goods only satisfied them indirectly. (For example, an apple might be a consumption good to a hungry man, while an apple seed would be a production good.) If we insist on a two-fold scheme, then money must be a production good, since it is clearly not a consumption good. Yet this is problematic too, because money is very different from other types of production goods.

A solution is to adopt a three-fold system, consisting of consumption goods, production goods, and media of exchange. This makes sense, because money is not a "commercial tool" in the same way that account books are. Although in a certain sense money "facilitates commerce" just as boats and railroads do, they differ in a crucial way: Increasing the supply of money does not make the community richer, whereas having more boats, railroads, and other production goods allows for the greater satisfaction of human desires. This is why money should be classified in a separate category, namely media of exchange.

## 2. Money as Part of Private Capital

**Private capital** can be defined as the aggregate of the products that serve as a means to the acquisition of goods. Money should clearly be included in this category, and in fact historically an interest-bearing sum of money was the starting point of the concept of "capital."

Over time, theorists realized that money was "barren" and did not directly yield its "fruits" the way physical seeds or human labor could. To explain why people would be willing to pay interest on money loans, we must recognize that money can be *exchanged* for other, productive goods. This observation reinforces the decision to classify money as a medium of exchange, rather than a production good: the only way to salvage the inclusion of money as a part of private capital, is to *distinguish* it from other production goods and recognize its special ability to be exchanged for them.

## 3. Money Not a Part of Social Capital

**Social (or productive) capital** can be defined as the aggregate of the products intended for employment in further production. If we deny that money is a production good, then obviously it cannot be a part of social (or productive) capital.

## *Important Contributions*

- Mises's summaries of various debates (on whether money is a production good, or whether it is part of social capital) may strike some readers as difficult or even tedious. However, in these passages Mises demonstrates his command of the literature, but also he explains *why* he favors one view over another. At times Mises differs from Eugen von Böhm-Bawerk, the great pioneer in (what we now call) Austrian economics after Menger. The reader can see that Mises is not simply following in the path laid out by his predecessors in the Austrian tradition, but instead weighs the arguments by various thinkers, and builds the Misesian system with the strongest components of each.

- As with his classification of money substitutes, credit money, etc., in this chapter Mises exercises great precision in defining his concepts and justifying his decisions. For the issues in this chapter, Mises tells the reader (p. 86) that the groundwork will be important for understanding the discussion of the **equilibrium and money rates of interest**, which will occur in part III of the book.

## *New Terminology*

**Equilibrium rate of interest:** The rate of interest corresponding to the true supplies of capital goods and consumer preferences for present versus future consumption. Also known as the natural rate of interest.

**Money rate of interest:** The rate of interest determined in the marketplace for loans of money. (The money rate can deviate from the equilibrium [or natural] rate of interest, in a process that is explained in part III of the book.)

**Private capital:** The aggregate of the products that serve as a means to the acquisition of goods.

**Social (productive) capital:** The aggregate of the products intended for employment in further production.

## *Study Questions*

1. What are the views of Roscher and Knies with respect to classifying money? (p. 79)

2. What was Helfferich's objection to those (like Knies) who wanted to deny that a monetary exchange was an act of production? (pp. 79–80)

3. Explain: "Money is obviously not a 'commercial tool' in the same sense as account books, exchange lists, the Stock Exchange, or the credit system." (p. 83)

4. Explain: "[W]hereas the changes in the value of . . . production goods and consumption goods do not mitigate the loss or reduce the gain of satisfaction resulting from . . . changes in their quantity, . . . changes in the value of money are accommodated in such a way to the demand for it that, despites increase or decreases in its quantity, the economic position of mankind remains the same." (p. 85)

5. What hindered the development of a scientific understanding of capital and interest? (pp. 88–89)

CHAPTER 6

# THE ENEMIES OF MONEY

*Chapter Outline*

## 1. Money in the Socialist Community

If a socialist society completely abolishes all property rights and distributes scarce goods and services according to a central plan, then there is no scope for even direct exchange (let alone indirect exchange) and therefore no room for money.

However, some socialist visionaries concede that even in their ideal society, people would retain ownership rights in personal consumption goods such as cigarettes, apples, loaves of bread, sweaters, and so forth. In this case, people would naturally engage in mutually beneficial trades, and ultimately would foster the development of money.

## 2. Money Cranks

Throughout the ages, reformers have blamed money for social ills. (The love of money is famously declared to be the root of all evil.) The hostility to gold and silver is particularly intense. Yet these reformers never explain their full vision of a world *without* money, for if they attempted such a description, the problems with their schemes would be obvious.

Other critics do not call for the abolition of money per se, but merely for an "elastic credit system," which expands or contracts the money supply according to the community's "need for currency." According to this particular group of **money cranks**, the current money and banking system imposes an artificial scarcity by restricting credit and charging higher interest rates than necessary.

## *Technical Notes*

- Some socialists viewed money itself as a "dirty" product of the market economy, and believed that in a pure socialist society, there would be no need for it. However, as Mises explains, some of the more sophisticated theorists imagined that the workers in a socialist community would have property rights in consumption goods (and perhaps personal tools of the trade for skilled artisans etc.). However, what *cannot* be allowed in a socialist community—lest it become a system of capitalism—is private ownership in the large-scale means of production, such as farmland, factories, railroads, etc.

- Mises concedes that a socialist community that retained private ownership in personal consumption goods, could foster the emergence of genuine money. However, Mises is *not* here referring to the "labor certificates" envisioned by some socialist theorists. For example, we could imagine that socialist factory and farm managers hand out one certificate for every labor hour (of suitable quality) that each worker performs. Then, once the "crop" of output goods has been "harvested" from all the various factories and farms—including not just bottles of milk but also television sets and basketballs—the socialist leaders determine what fraction of the crop each certificate entitles the bearer to, based on the size of the harvest and the total number of certificates that were issued. Although many casual observers think that this is basically what money *is*—a claim on the "real output" of society—such a view is very superficial. Actual money (as opposed to a money substitute) is not a claim on anything; it is its own good, but of course it is valued because of its expected purchasing power. If a fire destroys half of the crop, then the labor certificates will necessarily entitle their holders to one-half as much. But with one unit of money, it is not necessarily true that its exchange value in the market would drop by exactly one-half, and in any event the processes governing its purchasing power are completely different from those governing the "redemption power" of a labor certificate in a socialist community.

- When dealing with the last category of "money cranks" on page 94, Mises explains that the mainstream economists of his day could not effectively refute those who claimed that a massive expansion of the money supply—in order to drive the interest rate down to zero—would bring about material abundance. Although most economists and practical businessmen shied away from such extreme proposals, they were merely the logical extension of the prevailing economic doctrines concerning money and banking. It would take Mises's own work, in particular his development of the **circulation credit theory of the trade cycle**, to adequately explode this variety of monetary crankishness.

## *New Terminology*

**Circulation credit theory of the trade cycle:** The theory developed by Mises (in the present book) explaining the boom phase of the business cycle as due to the artificial expansion of bank credit, made possible by fiduciary media. The bust is then inevitable, as capital goods are malinvested during the boom.

**Money cranks:** Very naïve writers who believe that scarcity is an artificial institutional constraint, and that prosperity requires only a sufficient willingness to create more money and/or issue more bank credit.

## *Study Questions*

1. What two trends cause the emergence of indirect exchange to become inevitable? (p. 91)

2. Would the isolated household use money? Why or why not? (p. 91)

3. Do all socialists propose the complete abolition of money? (p. 91)

4. If the amount of "real output"—number of apples, TVs, heart surgeries, etc.—were to fall in half, would the purchasing power of money necessarily fall in half? (p. 92)

5. Does Mises endorse the banking theories of Tooke and Fullarton? (p. 94)

PART II

# THE VALUE OF MONEY

CHAPTER 7

# THE CONCEPT OF THE VALUE OF MONEY

## *Summary*

The main task of economic theory is to explain money's *objective* exchange value, or what is often called the *purchasing power of money*. This refers to the amount of goods that someone can obtain in the marketplace with a unit of money. This explanation in turn ultimately goes back to *subjective* valuations.

What sets money apart from all other goods is that money is useful (and hence valuable) to people *only* because of its purchasing power. In its capacity as a medium of exchange, a unit of money is only useful inasmuch as it can be used to acquire *other* goods and services.

When we say a particular good has objective exchange value, the term "objective" is *not* used to mean that this value inherently resides in the object. All market prices are ultimately determined by subjective human preferences, and therefore are subject to change whenever people's valuations change. A typical good's "objective" exchange value is still determined by the subjective use-values of the end user. (For example, a car manufacturer will produce cars based not on his personal whims, but on how much he can charge for them in the market. Yet these prices themselves are due to how much his customers enjoy driving the various vehicles.)

The one essential difference with money is that it *has no* subjective use-value, which could ultimately explain its objective exchange value. Its *only* value—*qua* money—derives from its ability to exchange for other goods in the market. This is why applying modern subjective value theory to the explanation of objective money prices is such a tricky affair. Those economists of Mises's day who tried to explain the purchasing power of money based solely on its industrial applications, were completely evading the issue. In particular, they would be helpless to explain the purchasing power of fiat money.

## *Chapter Outline*

### 1. Subjective and Objective Factors in the Theory of the Value of Money

When it comes to money, the main task of economic theory is to explain its *objective* exchange value, or what is often called the *purchasing power of money*. This refers to the amount of goods that someone can obtain in the marketplace with a unit of money. This is an *objective* fact: if Tom sees that a dollar bill can purchase three postage stamps, then Bill will observe the same purchasing power as well.

Even though economics focuses on the explanation of money's objective exchange value, the explanation itself ultimately goes back to *subjective* valuations. For the economist grounded in the modern subjective value theory (developed by Carl Menger and his followers), *all* prices in the market must be explained by reference to individuals' subjective valuations. This rule holds even for money.

What sets money apart from all other goods is that money is useful (and hence valuable) to people *only* because of its purchasing power. In its capacity as a medium of exchange, a unit of money is only useful inasmuch as it can be used to acquire *other* goods and services.

When it comes to explaining the price of, say, an original painting by Picasso, the economist starts with the fact that some people place a very high subjective value on holding such artwork. The economist has no obligation to explain *why* people enjoy the mere possession of a canvas covered in paint; he or she takes this preference as a given, and proceeds to explain the exchange value of the Picasso in the marketplace. Yet when it comes to money, the economist can't explain its "price" (i.e., purchasing power) merely by saying that people enjoy acquiring and holding cash balances. Such an argument—by itself—would be circular, because the *reason* people want to hold cash balances is that money has purchasing power. That is why explaining the "price" of money is a much subtler task than explaining the price of a Picasso.

## 2. The Objective Exchange Value of Money

The objective exchange value of goods can be defined as "their objective significance in exchange" or "their capacity in given circumstances to procure a specific quantity of other goods as an equivalent in exchange." Nowadays we might use the term **market value** to express the same concept as objective exchange value.

When we say a particular good has objective exchange value, the term "objective" is *not* used to mean that this value inherently resides in the object. (In other words, we are not using the term the same way that a good might have an objective weight or color.) All market prices are ultimately determined by subjective human preferences, and therefore are subject to change whenever people's valuations change. But a good's market value is still "objective" in the sense that any individual can take it as a given fact.

The **objective exchange value of money** refers to the possibility of obtaining a certain quantity of other goods in exchange for the money, while the **price of money** is this actual quantity of other goods. (The terms are not identical, but are very similar, as Mises explains on page 101.)

## 3. The Problems Involved in the Theory of the Value of Money

In modern economies, producers as a rule evaluate their output on the basis of subjective exchange value, rather than subjective use-value. For example, the owner of an automobile factory doesn't order his employees to produce cars that he himself wants to drive. On the contrary, he instructs his employees to make cars that he plans on *selling* to others, based on what his customers want to drive. When formulating his business plans, then, he is guided by his personal, *subjective* valuations of the other goods he will be able to buy (houses, fancy meals, yachts, etc.) with the revenues from the sale of his cars.

In order for the owner of the automobile factory (and other producers) to accurately envision the tradeoffs of different production decisions, he needs to know the *objective* exchange value of the various cars he could manufacture. It's not enough that the car producer knows that he values yachts and steak dinners; he also needs to know how much money he can raise by selling different models of his cars, and how much money he will need to spend if he wants to acquire yachts and steak dinners. Thus most production decisions involve a complex interdependence on both subjective and objective valuations.

The one essential difference with money is that it *has no* subjective use-value, which could ultimately explain its objective exchange value. In contrast, when it comes to the automobiles, yachts, and steak dinners, the economist ultimately could explain their relative exchange values (i.e., how many automobiles would trade for one yacht, etc.) by reference to individuals' subjective use-values from them (i.e., how much people liked driving cars, versus piloting yachts or eating steak).

But with money, its *only* value—*qua* money—derives from its ability to exchange for other goods in the market. This is why applying modern subjective value theory to the explanation of objective money prices is such a tricky affair. Those economists of Mises's day who tried to explain the purchasing power of money based solely on its industrial applications, were completely evading the issue. In particular, they would be helpless to explain the purchasing power of fiat money.

## *Technical Notes*

- In the beginning of this chapter, Mises spends time placing his analysis of money within the framework of subjective value theory, as it had been developed by his Austrian predecessors (notably Menger, Böhm-Bawerk, and Wieser). Some of the terminology may appear quaint to modern economists, even those who have studied Austrian economics. But to properly explain the process by which subjective individual valuations generate objective market prices, it is necessary to distinguish between **use-value** and **exchange value**, and these concepts in turn both come with a subjective and an objective dimension. For example, the objective use-value of a pig would include the collection of bacon strips it could physically yield, while the objective use-value of a tomato seed would include the tomatoes it could physically yield. These would be empirical facts, not subject to opinion. However, a vegetarian would probably assign a lower *subjective* use-value to the pig than to the tomato seed, while a meat-lover might do the opposite. On the other hand, *both* the vegetarian and the meat-lover would agree that the *objective exchange* value of the pig is much higher than that of the tomato seed. For example, it would be an indisputable fact that the pig could fetch more grams of gold (or dollar bills) than the tomato seed, if both were put up for sale.

- Applying these concepts to money, Mises explains (pp. 97–98) that there are two acceptable ways of making an important point. One way is to claim that money's subjective use-value is the same as its subjective exchange-value. (That is, the significance that a particular individual attributes to a quantity of money, must be the same significance that he or she attributes to the goods for which the money can be exchanged, because the money can't be used to satisfy wants directly.) A different way to make the point is to say that money *has no* use-value at all, because any value it possesses necessarily derives from its exchange value. Mises doesn't take a position on which of these alternate descriptions is better; he merely wants to stress the fundamental point that people consider money useful and valuable *only* because they expect to use it to acquire other goods. (Of course Mises is talking about money *qua* money. A bar of gold, for example, can still possess use-value for its industrial or ornamental applications.)

## *New Terminology*

**Exchange value:** The significance of a good due to its ability to be traded for other goods. (Exchange value can be qualified as either subjective or objective.)

**Market value:** Synonymous with the objective exchange value of a good, typically quoted in money terms.

**Objective exchange value of money:** The possibility of obtaining a certain quantity of other goods in exchange for a unit of money.

**Price of money:** The quantity of goods (or services) that must be given up in exchange to acquire a unit of money.

**Use-value:** The significance of a good due to its ability to be directly used by the owner in consumption or production. (Use-value can be qualified as either subjective or objective.)

## *Study Questions*

1. What is the central element in the economic problem of money? (p. 97)

2. Does the subjective theory of value apply to the case of money, as to all other goods? (p. 97)

3. Explain: "In the case of money, subjective use-value and subjective exchange value coincide." (p. 97)

4. Explain: "It should be observed that even objective exchange value is not really a property of the goods themselves, bestowed on them by nature. . . ." (p. 100)

5. If money (e.g., gold) has an industrial use as well as a monetary use, what will be the relation between its objective exchange values in those two different applications? (pp. 104–05)

CHAPTER 8

# THE DETERMINANTS OF THE OBJECTIVE EXCHANGE VALUE, OR PURCHASING POWER, OF MONEY

## *Summary*

The usefulness of money derives solely from its purchasing power. Therefore, today's valuation of money is dependent on its purchasing power *yesterday*, which in turn was influenced by money's purchasing power two days ago. Such reasoning does not lead to an infinite regress, because at some point in the past we arrive at the state of direct exchange, when goods were only valued for their direct use. This theory of the origin of money is the only one compatible with a subjectivist explanation.

The historical continuity in the value of money distinguishes it from all other commodities. People do not derive their utility from apples or oranges based on their prices, but people *do* evaluate the usefulness of a quantity of money based on its purchasing power.

The problem with many rival theories of the purchasing power of money—such as a simple quantity theory or "supply and demand" explanation—is that they have to take the value of money as given, and can only explain *deviations* from this stipulated starting point. They can't explain the *absolute* level of money-prices, i.e., they can't explain the actual exchange ratio between money and other goods at a particular time. The subjectivist, marginal-utility theory developed by Menger and his successors *can* explain the precise, absolute money-prices of the market today.

The exchange ratio between money and all other goods—in other words, the purchasing power of money—may be affected by changes in people's valuations of the money side *or* the (other) commodities side of the ratio.

In its crudest form, the quantity theory of money is obviously wrong: It is simply not true that, say, a doubling in the quantity of money will lead to an exact doubling of all prices (quoted in money).

Modern value theory must explain the demand to hold money by starting with the subjective preferences of the individual. The community's demand to hold money is simply the summation of the individual demands. No individual can make use of the popular "macro" approaches, which employ formulas involving "total volume of transactions" and "velocity of circulation." Economists therefore should not use such concepts when explaining the purchasing power of money.

**Money certificates** are money substitutes that are fully "covered" by money proper, while **fiduciary media** are money substitutes that are issued above the redemption fund.

## *Chapter Outline*

# I. THE ELEMENT OF CONTINUITY IN THE OBJECTIVE EXCHANGE VALUE OF MONEY

## 1. The Dependence of the Subjective Valuation of Money on the Existence of Objective Exchange Value

In order for individuals to evaluate the subjective value of money, they must first consider its usefulness which is derived solely from its purchasing power. In this sense, today's valuation of money is dependent on people's observations of its purchasing power *yesterday*. And yesterday's purchasing power, in turn, was influenced by money's purchasing power two days ago.

Such reasoning does not lead to an *infinite* regress, because at some point in the past we arrive at the state of direct exchange, when goods were only valued for their direct use. At that time, goods such as gold and silver—which would become money, down the road—were valued exclusively for their industrial and ornamental purposes.

## 2. The Necessity for a Value Independent of the Monetary Function Before an Object can Serve as Money

The previous discussion has established that in order for individuals to place a value upon money, they must have some basis for forecasting its future purchasing power. The only way they can do this, is if the money good already has a history of objective exchange value, which the individuals can consult.

This reasoning shows the flaw in the myths about the creation of money being due to a social pact. Rather, Menger's theory of the origin of money—in which the money commodities were originally used as ordinary commodities—is the only one compatible with a subjectivist explanation.

## 3. The Significance of Pre-Existing Prices in the Determination of Market Exchange Ratios

The historical continuity in the value of money distinguishes it from all other commodities. It is true that there appears to be "inertia" with respect to exchange ratios between goods; if 2 apples trade for 1 orange on Tuesday, it is unlikely that 20 apples will trade for 1 orange on Wednesday. But it is not true that Tuesday's exchange ratio somehow influences Wednesday's. Rather, the underlying determinants of Tuesday's price (such as people's subjective preferences for the two fruits) probably will not change very much by Wednesday.

In contrast, economic theory *does* need to rely on Tuesday's purchasing power of money, in order to explain Wednesday's purchasing power of money. People do not derive their utility from apples or oranges based on their prices, but people *do* evaluate the usefulness of a quantity of money based on its purchasing power.

## 4. The Applicability of the Marginal-Utility Theory to Money

The problem with many rival theories of the purchasing power of money—such as a simple quantity theory or "supply and demand" explanation—is that they have to take the value of money as given, and can only explain *deviations* from this stipulated starting point. For example, it is correct to say, "If a car originally has a price of $1,000, then an increase in the stock of money will, other things equal, lead to a new car price that is higher than $1,000."

Yet this isn't really a full explanation; why wasn't the car's original price $10, or $100,000? The simple "supply and demand" approach—correct as far as it goes—by itself can't explain the *absolute* level of money-prices, i.e., it can't explain the actual exchange ratio between money and other goods at a particular time.

The subjectivist, marginal-utility theory developed by Menger and his successors *can* explain the precise, absolute money-prices of the market today, just as it can explain the precise exchange ratios between apples and oranges.

At first it appears that money is a peculiar case that cannot be handled this way, because people's marginal utility of money is itself derived from its objective purchasing power. But once we introduce the time element, we are *not* arguing in a circle. We are explaining *today's* purchasing power of money by reference to *yesterday's* purchasing power, and so on. We can logically follow the chain all the way back in time, until the point at which the money commodity was valued solely for its nonmonetary uses, i.e., before it became a medium of exchange.

## 5. "Monetary" and "Nonmonetary" Influences Affecting the Objective Exchange Value of Money

The preceding sections have established the *origin* of the value of money. (Namely, subjective marginal utility analysis—coupled with Menger's explanation of the origin of money—can explain today's absolute level of the purchasing power of money.) It is now acceptable to focus on the laws or principles governing *changes* in the value of money. Economists usually start at this step, even though logically they should have explained the original value of money first.

The exchange ratio between two goods can be affected by changes in the valuation for just one of the goods. For example, on Tuesday Jim may choose to drink soda over cough medicine.

But on Wednesday he may reverse his preferences, and choose the medicine over the soda. This obviously needn't be due to Jim's sudden distaste for soda.

In the same way, the exchange ratio between money and all other goods—in other words, the purchasing power of money—may be affected by changes in people's valuations of the money side *or* the (other) commodities side of the ratio.

# II. FLUCTUATIONS IN THE OBJECTIVE EXCHANGE VALUE OF MONEY EVOKED BY CHANGES IN THE RATIO BETWEEN THE SUPPLY OF MONEY AND THE DEMAND FOR IT

## 6. The Quantity Theory

In its crudest form, the **quantity theory of money** is obviously wrong: It is simply not true that, say, a doubling in the quantity of money will lead to an exact doubling of all prices (quoted in money).

The germ of truth in the historical expositions of the quantity theory is that a connection exists between variations in the value of money on the one hand, and variations in the relations between the demand for money and the supply of it on the other. Throughout history, writers have noted the patterns, but the task for the modern economist is to express these truisms with the tools of modern subjective value theory.

## 7. The Stock of Money and the Demand for Money

Modern value theory must explain the demand to hold money by starting with the subjective preferences of the individual. The community's demand to hold money is simply the summation of the individual demands. No individual can make use of the popular "macro" approaches, which employ formulas involving "total volume of transactions" and "velocity of circulation." Economists therefore should not use such concepts when explaining the purchasing power of money.

In certain cases it is useful to distinguish between the individual's demand to hold money in the broader sense versus money in the narrower sense. The former is the individual's demand to hold both money and money substitutes (i.e., perfectly secure and immediate claims on money). The latter is the individual's demand to hold money proper.

**Money certificates** are money substitutes that are fully "covered" by money proper, while **fiduciary media** are money substitutes that are issued above the redemption fund. For example, if a particular commercial bank accepts 1,000 ounces of gold in deposits which it keeps in the vault, but issues 1,100 paper banknotes entitling the bearer to an ounce of gold upon presentation, then 1,000 of the notes are money certificates, while 100 are fiduciary media. (In commercial practice the notes are indistinguishable, and so we can say that about 91 percent of a given note is "covered" while the remainder is "unbacked.")

## 8. The Consequences of an Increase in the Quantity of Money While the Demand for Money Remains Unchanged or Does Not Increase to the Same Extent

A crude, mechanical version of the quantity theory of money holds that a doubling of the stock of money will lead to a uniform doubling of the money prices of all other goods and services. The logic behind such a view rests on the true observation that any given quantity of money can perform all the services of money for the community, with the appropriate "price level." For example, we can imagine two economies side-by-side, which are equal in all ways except that the second community has twice the amount of money as the first. It is clear that in the second community, the prices of all goods and services have to be exactly double their values in the first community, in order to render these economies equal in all "real" respects.

Yet from this thought experiment, we *cannot* conclude that if we started with the first community, and then magically doubled everyone's holding of money, that we would end up with the second community. For one thing, different individuals would respond differently to the increase in their holdings of money. Everyone would of course revise downward his or her marginal utility for a unit of money—because the stock in possession increased—but these downward movements would not be equal for all people. Because the marginal unit of money would be less valuable than before the magical increase, people would now go out and buy more goods, tending to push up prices. But different people would increase their purchases in different ways, and (in any realistic scenario) would push up the prices of some goods more than others.

Another complication is that in the real world, new influxes of money do not magically augment the cash balances of everyone in the community proportionally. Instead, new money enters the community through increased holdings of a small group of people (such as the owners of gold mines, or the customers who borrow money from a bank issuing fiduciary media). Thus the new money ripples out into the economy, as the first recipients spend the new money, then the second recipients spend it, and so on.

Nobody would ever be so foolish as to claim that, say, a doubling of the quantity of sugar would lead to an exact halving of the exchange ratio of sugar against all other goods and services. Yet that is precisely what the crude Quantity Theorists assert when it comes to money.

## 9. Criticism of Some Arguments Against the Quantity Theory

Although in its crude form, the quantity theory is erroneous, even so we can defend it from some invalid objections. For example, some writers object that the quantity theory only holds *ceteris paribus* (i.e., when "other things are held equal"). Yet this is hardly a good objection against the quantity theory, since a critic could say the same thing about *any* law or principle in economic science.

Another objection people have raised against the quantity theory is that its predictions are in actual practice nullified by the behavior of "**hoards**." For example, the critic of the quantity theory might say that a large influx of new money *won't* have a tendency to push up prices, because some people in the community will simply expand their holdings of cash. On the other hand, say these critics, if the demand to hold money (for reasons of commerce) should suddenly increase, this won't lead to a fall in prices (as the quantity theory would predict), because the hoards will release some of their cash into the community to satisfy the new demand.

The fundamental problem with this view is that economically, there is no distinction between the normal demand to hold cash versus "hoarding." At any moment in time, *every* unit of money in the community is in someone's cash balance; there is no such thing as money "in circulation" that could be contrasted with money "sitting idle."

The money held by a hoarder performs the same economic function as the money held by a normal businessperson; they are both holding the money because they expect to achieve greater satisfactions from what it can buy in the future, than from what it could buy in the present. Because of uncertainty, people do not necessarily "earmark" every unit of money for a particular future purchase. Nonetheless, when we analyze *why* people hold money at all, we realize that there is no qualitative difference between the hoarder and the nonhoarder. All hoarding really means, is that someone carries cash balances larger than his peers'.

## 10. Further Applications of the Quantity Theory

Generally speaking, the demand for money increases over time, due to population increases and the intensification of the division of labor (and hence the need for exchange transactions). For this reason, it was only a theoretical curiosity for economists to try to explain what would happen if the demand for money fell, while the stock of money remained the same.

If we were to mechanically apply the quantity theory to such a situation, we would conclude that prices would rise (i.e., the purchasing power of money would fall) uniformly, in direct proportion to the drop in demand for money. However, a more satisfactory explanation needs to take into account the subjective valuations of individuals. Rather than focusing merely on crude aggregates, it is better to analyze the scenario by saying that when the demand for money falls (while the stock of it remains constant), individuals discover that they are holding larger cash balances than they desire. To improve their position, they seek to exchange some of their excess cash holdings for other goods or services. In doing so, they push up the prices of these items.

Eventually, the fall in money's purchasing power reduces the "real" size of an individual's cash balance until he is happy with it. If everyone in the community decides he or she is holding "too much money," the only way to restore equilibrium is for prices to rise. If one person reduces his cash balance by spending, the seller necessarily increases his cash balance by the same amount. The given stock of money is rearranged among the people in the community;

per capita cash balances have to remain the same. Even so, the rise in prices can satisfy everyone's desire to hold smaller cash balances, because cash is held for the purpose of acquiring other goods and services. People evaluate the size of their cash holdings in terms of its purchasing power, not really by how many units of money they possess.

Although historically the demand for money itself generally grows—except perhaps for financial crises—there are cases where the demand for particular *kinds* of money may fall dramatically. A notable example is the demonetization of silver. As this precious metal ceased being used as a medium of exchange, and became valued solely for its industrial and ornamental applications, its exchange value fell.

## III. A SPECIAL CAUSE OF VARIATIONS IN THE OBJECTIVE EXCHANGE VALUE OF MONEY ARISING FROM THE PECULIARITIES OF INDIRECT EXCHANGE

### 11. "Dearness of Living"

Thus far in the chapter the analysis of the objective exchange value of money has only relied on determinants that could have just as well been applied to *any* commodity, not just the commonly accepted medium of exchange (i.e., the money commodity). In contrast, section III examines possible changes in the objective exchange value of money that can only apply because it is a medium of exchange. The context of the discussion is the layperson's complaint of the "dearness of living," meaning that every generation prices seem to be higher than before.

## 12. Wagner's Theory: The Influence of the Permanent Predominance of the Supply Side over the Demand Side on the Determination of Prices

Wagner explains the general rise in prices—or what is the same thing, the general fall in the purchasing power of a unit of money—by the alleged superior power of the "supply side" of the economy. The sellers of goods and services stand more to gain from price hikes than their customers stand to lose, because the price of beef (say) affects the livelihood of the butcher far more than it affects the fortunes of the average household. Wagner's theory is flawed, however, because it cannot easily incorporate the fact that retail prices must also respond to changes in wholesale prices.

## 13. Wieser's Theory: The Influence on the Value of Money Exerted by a Change in the Relations Between Natural Economy and Money Economy

Wieser attempts to explain the persistent rise in prices over time by the gradual transformation of a "Natural Economy" into a "Money Economy." As more and more people and regions are brought into the practice of monetary exchange, Wieser argues that certain things that were previously handled through home production must now be included in the final price of goods intended for market. Wieser offers a specific example of the prices of milk and eggs rising in a rural village, once the villagers become involved with frequent trade with the much larger town. However, Wieser ignores the obvious flip-side of the development: the prices of milk and eggs will be lower *in the town* because of the new source of supply. The integration of the rural village into the monetary nexus gives no reason for a general rise in prices, it merely explains why the gap in prices (between the town and village) should be whittled away.

## 14. The Mechanism of the Market as a Force Affecting the Objective Exchange Value of Money

In direct exchange, if a potential buyer believes that the asking price of the seller is too high, the exchange will not occur. However, with the use of money, there is another possible outcome, that seems to happen in the real world. The buyer may go ahead and pay a price (in money) that he originally deemed "too high," but will compensate by increasing the asking price for the goods that *he* has to sell. Thus wage earners might acquiesce in higher food prices, yet demand pay increases from their employers. The employers, in turn, might agree, knowing that they will raise prices themselves.

None of this discussion renders the basic theory of price determination invalid. It merely underscores that with the special case of money, peculiar situations can affect its valuation that simply cannot occur in the case of direct exchange.

# IV. EXCURSUSES

## 15. The Influence of the Size of the Monetary Unit and Its Subdivisions on the Objective Exchange Value of Money

It is often asserted that the size of the monetary unit can affect its purchasing power, i.e., the general height of prices. In regard to wholesale prices, this is clearly absurd: merchants would adjust their large-scale transactions to achieve their desires, regardless of the unit.

However, there is some truth to the assertion when it comes to retail trade. For practical reasons, everyday purchases that have very low prices compared to most other goods (such as letter postage or pieces of fruit) must correspond somewhat to the lowest available denomination of the money. The use of token coinage (which can represent fractions of the standard monetary unit) and money substitutes, as well as the practice of selling multiple units of goods (e.g., a dozen eggs) as a package, can provide a wide range of flexibility, but even so it must be admitted that the size of the monetary unit does have an influence on prices quoted at the retail level.

## 16. A Methodological Comment

In a review of the first edition of the book, Professor Walter Lotz defended Laughlin from the critique leveled by Mises (on pages 125–28 in the present edition of the book). To review, Laughlin had tried to explain the value of paper gulden (which for a time were not redeemable in precious metal) by the prospect of their eventual redemption. Mises examined the discount investors placed on bonds issued by the same government and concluded that there must be some other factor at work, to explain the premium investors placed on the paper gulden. The answer, of course, was that the paper gulden were used as money, whereas the bonds were not. Therefore the paper gulden were valued on account of their use as media of exchange.

Lotz defends Laughlin by referring to statements from influential figures that they truly did speculate on the eventual redemption of the paper gulden. Mises points out that this entirely misses the point of his critique: Even if it is admitted that the paper gulden would eventually be redeemable for gold, that fact wouldn't explain why the notes traded at a premium to bonds issued by the same government. More generally, Lotz approaches economic problems not through theoretical reasoning, but by appeal to historical circumstances, a procedure that Mises rejects on methodological grounds.

## *Important Contributions*

- On page 108, Mises alludes to Menger and Böhm-Bawerk's explanations of how prices are determined in direct exchanges (i.e., what most people call "barter"). For example, suppose people in a community own horses, and others own cows. Each person will rank various units of each animal on his own subjective scale of values. Bill might consider his first horse as the most important animal, then his first cow, and then his second horse. John, in contrast, might consider his first and then second cows to occupy the highest- and second-highest ranks in his scale of values, while his first horse comes in at the third slot. (Note that everyone exhibits diminishing marginal utility in each animal.) People will trade horses for cows so long as there are mutually beneficial trades; perhaps Bill will trade his 17th and 18th cows for John's 6th horse, because such a trade makes both men better off in their own subjective views. (In this case, the "price" of one horse is two cows.) To understand the description Mises gives to the range of possible market prices under bilateral competition, the reader should consult the numerical example in Murray Rothbard, *Man, Economy, and State* (scholar's edition, 2nd edition; Auburn, Ala.: Mises Institute, 2009, pp. 106–26).

- The first sections of this chapter lay out Mises's famous **regression theorem**, which successfully applies subjective value theory to the case of money. Earlier economists had been unable to accomplish this feat, because they thought the approach would lead to a circular argument in the case of money. (How can we explain the objective purchasing power of money by reference to subjective valuations, when those subjective valuations in turn are completely dependent on money's objective purchasing power? It seemed to Mises's predecessors that this approach said, "Money is valuable because money is valuable.") Mises broke out of the circularity by introducing the time element: People are willing to sell other goods and services for money *today* because they expect that same money to command purchasing power *tomorrow*. (This explains money's purchasing power *today*.) But people's expectations about the future purchasing power of money are formed by their observations of the recent past, i.e., their observations of money's purchasing power *yesterday*. We can push the explanation all the way back until the point at which (commodity) money had an objective exchange value due entirely to its use in nonmonetary applications.

- On page 160 Mises gives a simple illustration (involving a pear, lemonade, etc.) of how an individual's scale of values can be transformed with the possibility of market exchange.

## *New Terminology*

**Quantity theory of money:** An old doctrine explaining changes in the purchasing power of money by reference to the quantity of money and the demand to hold it. (There are many versions of the quantity theory, with the more mechanical ones—which posit that a doubling of the money stock will lead to a doubling of all prices—being obviously wrong.)

**Money certificates:** Money substitutes that are fully backed by money (in the narrower sense).

**Fiduciary media:** Money substitutes issued over and above the money (in the narrower sense) held in the redemption fund. Fiduciary media are "unbacked."

**Hoards (noun):** People who accumulate large cash balances in certain circumstances, allegedly counteracting the predictions of a naïve quantity theory of money.

**Regression Theorem:** Mises's argument that the current purchasing power of money is influenced by people's memory of yesterday's purchasing power. The causality is traced back in time, until the point at which the money good was valued as a regular commodity in direct exchange.

## *Study Questions*

1. Explain: "The subjective value of money must be measured by the marginal utility of the goods for which the money can be exchanged." (p. 109)

2. If all types of money must have originally had a *non*monetary source of valuation, how can Mises explain fiat money? (pp. 110–11)

3. If the "past value of money is taken over by the present," does that mean current conditions and expectations have no influence on the value of money today? (p. 111)

4. Explain: "If all the exchange ratios of the past were erased from human memory, the process of market-price-determination might certainly become more difficult . . . but it would not become impossible." (p. 113)

5. Explain: "[A] mechanical theory of price-determination was arrived at—a doctrine of Supply and Demand. . . . It is correct or incorrect, according to the content given to the words Supply and Demand." (pp. 128–29)

CHAPTER 9

# THE PROBLEM OF THE EXISTENCE OF LOCAL DIFFERENCES IN THE OBJECTIVE EXCHANGE VALUE OF MONEY

*Chapter Outline*

## 1. Interlocal Price Relations

Money can perform its services from virtually any location. Gold stored in the cellars of the Bank of England can be used as a common medium of exchange anywhere in the world, through the use of banknotes, checks, and **clearing systems**. In contrast, physical location is a crucial feature of other economic goods. "Coffee in Brazil" is not the same good as "coffee in England," from the perspective of English consumers.

If we completely disregard the possible (but small) influence of the position of money on its valuation, then we can derive the law that every economic good that is ready for consumption, has a subjective use-value *qua* consumption good at the place where it is, and *qua* production good at those places to which it may be transported for consumption. Therefore, the money-price of any commodity in any place must be the same as the money-price at any other place, once we adjust for the money-cost of transportation, unless there are institutional limits restricting exchange. (In the real world, there are possible costs of the transport of money, the need to re-coin it, and so on, that would affect the **foreign-exchange rate** such as the **cable rate**. These complications do not arise if we assume the money itself stays put.)

## 2. Alleged Local Differences in the Purchasing Power of Money

Despite the arguments put forward in the previous section, many people still cling to the belief that one's money "goes further" in some regions compared to others. However, this erroneous view neglects the fact that the same physical item is a different good, economically speaking, depending on its location. A cocktail in a bar in Manhattan is a different good from the "same drink" in a bar in Boise, so their different money-prices cannot lead us to conclude that the "value of money" is higher in Boise than in Manhattan. On the contrary, the purchasing power of money will tend to be equalized in all regions where it is used, and any apparent discrepancies are due to differences on the commodity side.

## 3. Alleged Local Differences in the Cost of Living

Closely related to the fallacy that the purchasing power of money can vary from region to region, is the claim that the "cost of living" is higher in one area versus another. Here too we need to consider the subjective valuations of individuals, rather than the physical attributes of goods and services. An apartment carries a higher rental price in a resort town near a popular beach, versus a rural area with no special attractions, precisely because people value the proximity to the beach, the local night life, etc. It is simply not true that the same lifestyle can be obtained more cheaply in the rural town than in the resort town. If the "cost of living" *really* were higher in one location, people would move out of the area until its prices had fallen enough to eliminate the discrepancy.

## *Technical Notes*

- Mises says on page 171 that the money-price of a commodity must be the same in all places, due account being made for the money-cost of transport, *and* disregarding "the time taken in transit." This caveat is necessary because the time dimension affects the subjective valuation of goods. For an extreme example, if it takes one year to ship a new computer to a colony on Mars, the manufacturer would insist on a higher retail price (obtainable in one year) than the current spot price on Earth, even after adding in explicit shipping expenses. This is because the computer manufacturer could receive revenues from Earth-based customers immediately, which is more valuable than having to wait a year to receive the same amount of money from Martian consumers.

- Mises concedes on pages 176–77 that there is a limited sense in which a region's higher "cost of living" is both valid theoretically and important in practice. Namely, for those workers who move to a region and do *not* subjectively value its amenities, the high money-prices for rent, parking, food, and so on must be compensated by an appropriate increase in their money-wages or salaries. For example, a hospital located in a resort beach town may need to offer a higher salary to attract (say) a qualified brain surgeon, if there happen to be no brain surgeons eager to live near the beach and who are therefore willing to accept the "normal" salary in the face of above-average prices for housing in the resort town.

## *New Terminology*

**Clearing systems:** Arrangements that cancel out or "clear" reciprocal financial claims, so that only net claims need be settled through the actual transfer of money.

**Foreign-exchange rate:** The exchange ratio between a domestic and foreign currency.

**Cable rate:** Slang used by foreign-exchange traders to denote the exchange rate between the U.S. dollar and British pound sterling.

## Study Questions

1. What complementary good is necessary to turn the production good "coffee in Brazil" into the consumption good "coffee in Europe"? (p. 171)

2. Explain: "To what absurd conclusions should we not come if we regarded goods lying in bond in a customs or excise warehouse and goods of the same technological species on which the duty or tax had already been paid as belonging to the same species of goods in the economic sense?" (pp. 172–73)

3. Explain: "It is hardly possible to agree with these arguments [put forward by Wieser], which smack a little too much of the cost-of-production theory of value and are certainly not to be reconciled with the principles of the subjective theory." (p. 174)

4. Can government restrictions on the movement of commodities and workers explain differences in retail prices? (p. 175)

5. What does Mises intend with his example of a hotel on the peaks and valleys of the Alps? (p. 176)

CHAPTER 10

# THE EXCHANGE RATIO BETWEEN MONEY OF DIFFERENT KINDS

## *Chapter Outline*

### 1. The Two-fold Possibility of the Coexistence of Different Kinds of Money

If the inhabitants of one country exclusively use a certain money (such as gold) for their domestic purchases, while a second country uses a different money (such as silver) for their domestic purchases, and the two countries are closely tied economically through trade, then it is incorrect to say that gold is the only common medium of exchange in the first country, and silver the only one in the second country. On the contrary, because merchants from one country can only trade goods with the other country's merchants through the use of the other domestic money, it is clear that both monies are media of exchange among people in both countries.

### 2. The Static or Natural Exchange Ratio between Different Kinds of Money

Whether two different monies operate side by side in the same country under a **parallel standard**, or whether one money is used exclusively for domestic trade in one country while the other money is likewise used in a second country, the same principle operates to regulate the exchange ratio (or what nowadays would be called the **exchange rate**) between the two monies. The theory of **purchasing power parity** says that the exchange ratio between two monies is determined by the respective exchange ratios of each money and other goods and services.

For example, if the price of a barrel of crude oil, measured in American dollars, is $100, while the price of a barrel of crude oil quoted in Japan is ¥8,000, then the exchange rate between the two currencies must be $1 for ¥80. If the exchange rate were different, there would be arbitrage opportunities for buying oil with one currency and selling it for the other. For example, suppose the exchange rate were $1 for ¥90 (rather than the equilibrium price of $1 for ¥80). In that case, a Japanese investor could take ¥8,000 and buy a barrel of crude oil. Then he could sell the oil to an American for $100. Finally he could go to the foreign exchange market and trade his $100 for ¥9,000. Thus the Japanese investor would have taken advantage of the existing price ratios to effortlessly turn his original ¥8,000 into ¥9,000. (His efforts to profit from this arbitrage opportunity would eventually eliminate it, since he would be acting to push up the yen-price of oil, push down the dollar-price of oil, and push down the yen-price of a dollar bill.)

If we first imagine a unified region using a single money, with no institutional obstacles to trade among its inhabitants, then it is clear that all commodities, including money, will be distributed among the population in accordance with marginal utility. If some people end up holding an above-average amount of (say) blankets, it is because their demand for this good is higher than average. By the same token, if some people acquire larger cash balances than others, it is because their demand to hold money is larger. There is no question of a dangerous "trade deficit" that could cause a "drain of money" from some people to others.

The same principles hold for nations. The aggregate figures of imports and exports are simply the summation of the trading activities between the individuals in each country. An accumulation of money in one country versus another can only be sustainable if the demand to hold money increases in the first country relative to the second. A trade deficit *not* accompanied by such a shift in the demand for money will be quickly self-reversing, as the prices in the country accumulating money will rise and the prices in the country losing money will fall.

## *Technical Notes*

- Mises argues on pages 179–80 that even in cases where the consumers in two different countries use different monies in everyday transactions, nonetheless if the regions are closely bound by international trade, then "from the economic point of view both [monies] must be regarded as money for each area." Updating to our times, what Mises has in mind is that the American businessman who wants to import cars from Japan, must at some point in the transaction exchange dollars for yen or vice versa. In that respect, the yen is a medium of exchange that is accepted in trade by the American businessman, in addition to all of the Japanese. However, it is still not obvious that this should mean that the yen is money even in the United States, because the definition of money is "a commonly accepted medium of exchange." To be sure, the yen is commonly accepted *among Americans doing business with Japan*, but it is not commonly accepted in the United States per se. However, the important point is not whether we say that the yen is money in the United States, but rather that we understand Mises's point that international trade requires businesspeople to accept the monies used in foreign lands.

- On page 182 Mises writes, "[Classical political economy] demonstrated that international movements of money are not consequences of the state of trade; that they constitute not the effect, but the cause, of a favourable or unfavourable trade-balance." He has in mind the following contrast in analysis: Suppose the English spend one million gold ounces importing wine from France, while the French spend only 900,000 gold ounces importing sweaters from England. An English mercantilist would probably bemoan the fact that his countrymen were importing more than they were exporting, and that this "unfavorable trade balance" was unwittingly losing 100,000 ounces of gold to the dastardly French. However, the classical economists such as Hume, Smith, and Ricardo could point out that the French (in the aggregate) apparently desired to increase their holdings of gold, while the English apparently desired to reduce their holdings. In that case, the only way to satisfy these shifts in money demand would be for the French to ship the English 100,000 gold ounces worth of goods, for which the English would not ship any (nonmonetary) goods in return.

## *New Terminology*

**Parallel Standard:** A monetary system in which two different goods both serve as monies. (For example, gold and silver might both serve as money under a Parallel Standard.)

**Exchange rate:** The ratio at which one currency trades against another in the foreign-exchange market.

**Purchasing Power Parity:** The theory stating that the exchange ratio between two monies is determined by the respective exchange ratios of each money and other goods and services.

## *Study Questions*

1. When England operated on a gold standard, while Germany operated on a silver standard, does Mises think that silver should have been considered as money even in England? (pp. 179–80)

2. How does the doctrine of purchasing power parity explain the exchange ratio between gold and silver in the example of cloth and wheat? (p. 181)

3. Explain: "If no other relations than those of barter exist between the inhabitants of two areas, then balances in favor of one party or the other cannot arise." (p. 182)

4. What was the train of thought that Mises says "dealt the Mercantilist Theory its death-blow"? (p. 182)

5. Explain: "[I]nternational movements of money, so far as they are not of a transient nature and consequently soon rendered ineffective by movements in the contrary direction, are always called forth by variations in the demand for money." (p. 185)

CHAPTER II

# THE PROBLEM OF MEASURING THE OBJECTIVE EXCHANGE VALUE OF MONEY AND VARIATIONS IN IT

## *Chapter Outline*

### 1. The History of the Problem

Some of the greatest minds in economics have devoted themselves to the development of indexes that would provide an objective measurement of the change in the purchasing power of money. However, such statistical techniques have never lived up to their promises, as even their own creators often admitted.

### 2. The Nature of the Problem

Just as we can express the price of any commodity by reference to how many units of money it takes to purchase one unit of the commodity, the opposite approach can yield the "price" of a unit of money in terms of the commodity. However, this technique yields as many "prices" of money as there are commodities. What economists desire is a method for combining all of this information into a single measurement of "the" purchasing power of money. Then, a second task is to ask of any *particular* commodity's price change, how much can be attributed to forces arising from the side of money (in contrast to a change in the relative scarcity of the good which would also make its price rise).

## 3. Methods of Calculating Index Numbers

Nearly all attempts at measuring the objective exchange value of money have relied on the assumption that if a large enough collection of goods are included in the "basket" to be measured, then changes in the relative scarcities of the goods themselves will largely cancel out. Thus the average or net change in the prices of *all* the goods (as quoted in money) will demonstrate whether the purchasing power of money has risen or fallen. Unfortunately, in practice it is only possible to carry out such calculations by making *ad hoc* assumptions about the relative importance of various factors. In the end, the economic theorist does not gain much from studying the various statistics of price movements that he could not obtain from deductive reasoning about the nature of exchange and money.

## 4. Wieser's Refinement of the Methods of Calculating Index Numbers

Wieser devised the most careful and satisfactory approach to measuring the objective exchange value of money, with a technique involving the contrast between nominal and real income. However, even Wieser's approach had several fatal flaws. For example, over large stretches of time, the types of income people could earn become incommensurable, robbing Wieser's technique of its desired precision.

## 5. The Practical Utility of Index Numbers

The criticisms leveled against various techniques for calculating index numbers refer to the problems of economic theory. In practical use for government policy, these techniques provide a rough guide to changes in the purchasing power of money.

## *Technical Notes*

- On page 189 Mises writes, "Invariability in respect of the property to be measured ... is a *sine qua non* of all measurement." For example, if a person is using a meter stick to measure length, then he must be assuming that the meter stick's length is itself invariable. Yet when economists try to measure changes in the objective exchange value of money (i.e., in the purchasing power of money), they run into the problem that there *are no* such invariable benchmarks. If the exchange ratio between money and any other commodity changes, it is not clear whether the change originates from the side of money or the commodity.

- Some numerical examples may clarify Mises's observations on index numbers (pp. 188–90). If the price of oil increases from $90 to $100, while the price of a television falls from $100 to $90, it is possible that these changes have nothing to do with the purchasing power of money, and merely reflect a shift in demand away from televisions and into oil. On the other hand, if *all* prices (quoted in money) in the community increased exactly by 10 percent in one year, then it would be clear that the purchasing power of money had fallen and was the driver of the price increases. But in the real world, things are never so clear-cut. Typically some prices rise while others fall, and the price movements are not in the same percentages across commodities. There is no nonarbitrary way to determine how much of a given good's change in price is due to changes in its relative value (with respect to other commodities) versus a change in the purchasing power of money.

## *Study Questions*

1. Explain: "Only by letting fall morsels of statistics is it possible for the economic theorist to maintain his prestige in the face of questions of this sort." (p. 188)

2. Explain: "He who cares to go to the trouble of demonstrating the uselessness of index numbers for monetary theory and the concrete tasks of monetary policy will be able to select a good proportion of his weapons from the writings of the very men who invented them." (p. 188)

3. Why are index numbers not very important for the "extension of the theory of the nature and value of money"? (pp. 189–90)

4. Even if we grant for the sake of argument that a loaf of bread possesses a constant utility in the objective sense of food value, why is this approach unhelpful when it comes to the use of index numbers in monetary theory? (p. 193)

5. Does Mises think that index numbers are completely useless? (p. 194)

CHAPTER 12

# THE SOCIAL CONSEQUENCES OF VARIATIONS IN THE OBJECTIVE EXCHANGE VALUE OF MONEY

*Chapter Outline*

## 1. The Exchange of Present Goods for Future Goods

People often exchange present goods for future goods, for example by lending money today (a present good) in exchange for a promise of repayment of future principal plus interest, or by agreeing today to exchange goods against money in the future. Although businesspeople take great caution regarding changes in the prices of *particular* commodities, they typically do not take into account the possible fall in the objective value of money itself. To the extent that people *do* protect themselves in contracts from possible changes in the value of a currency, it is only a paper currency the value of which might fall relative to a currency backed by gold. Hardly anyone (at the time of Mises's writing) realizes that the exchange value of gold itself could change during the length of a contract.

If changes in the purchasing power of money could be anticipated, then their impact could be offset by altering the terms of credit transactions. If both lenders and borrowers expect a weaker currency in the future (i.e., rising prices of most goods and services quoted in the currency), then lenders will insist on charging a higher interest rate and borrowers will be willing to pay it, because loans will be repaid in weaker currency.

## 2. Economic Calculation and Accountancy

Accountancy is imperfect in several respects. For example, it relies on subjective estimates of uncertain factors, such as the value of inventory (which is dependent on future demand) and the likelihood of default by the issuers of bonds. Yet another major flaw is that accountants use monetary figures as if they were akin to measures of length and weight. But since the purchasing power of money itself can change, accountancy is analogous to an architect designing blueprints in a world where rulers have variable lengths. Monetary depreciation can cause businesspeople to overestimate their profits and unwittingly engage in **capital consumption**.

## 3. Social Consequences of Variations in the Value of Money When Only One Kind of Money is Employed

If the quantity of a commodity such as coal is suddenly and unexpectedly increased, it will cause its price to drop. This will hurt those people who were holding large amounts of coal (such as the owners of coal mines and wholesalers) at the moment of the price drop, and it will help the consumers of coal (such as the owners of railroads and power plants). However, the gains will exceed the losses for the community as a whole, because the greater quantity of coal can yield more goods and services.

Things are different with the money commodity. Insofar as its *monetary* services are concerned, additional quantities confer no net benefits on the community. When new quantities of money enter the economy (from a new gold mine, for example), it spreads unevenly throughout the system. The chief beneficiaries are the original owners, then those upon whom they first spend the new money, and so on. The losers are those whose incomes (measured in money) do not rise even as they see prices going up in the things that they buy. Wealth is redistributed from some groups to others, but the community as a whole is not made richer by the influx of new money (except possibly indirectly if the beneficiaries of the inflation make more productive use of their redistributed wealth than the former owners).

## 4. The Consequences of Variations in the Exchange Ratio Between Two Kinds of Money

The uneven increase in prices due to an influx of new money (either from gold discoveries or from the issuance of more paper money and fiduciary media) can lead to redistribution even among groups using different currencies. For a modern example, suppose initially that one U.S. dollar trades for one euro, and that the price of a bushel of wheat initially is $5 and also €5. Then the Federal Reserve promises to sharply increase the quantity of dollars over the next few months, so that speculators on the foreign exchange market push down the value of the dollar so that it now trades for only one-half of a euro.

In this situation, the price of U.S. wheat would be €2.50 from the perspective of European millers, while wheat purchased from European farmers would be the original €5. The demand for American exported wheat would increase, while the American demand for European wheat would collapse. The prices of wheat in the two currencies would quickly adjust until balance had been restored, with U.S. wheat selling for (say) $8 and European wheat selling for €4. But even after this quick adjustment, there would be a lasting advantage given to American wheat exporters, because they could sell wheat for $8 instead of $5, even though their expenses (on labor, tractors, etc.) had not yet risen proportionally. European millers and consumers of bread would also benefit, because from their perspective the price of wheat would have fallen from €5 to €4 per bushel, even while their money incomes stayed the same. Two large groups of losers would be U.S. consumers and European wheat farmers. Only after all U.S. domestic prices had adjusted to the new quantity of dollars would the redistribution cease.

## *Technical Notes*

- On pages 195–96, Mises writes, "When anybody buys (or sells) corn, cotton, or sugar futures … he is well aware of the risks that are involved in the transaction. He will carefully weigh the chances of future variations in prices, and often take steps, by means of insurance or **hedging transactions** … to reduce the **aleatory** factor in his dealings." His purpose in this passage is to contrast the businessman's wariness concerning *individual* price changes over time, with the businessman's (at that time) ignorance of changes in the purchasing power of money over time. However, Mises's description is difficult to explain to a novice, because normally economists would describe the use of **futures contracts** as *themselves* "insurance" or "hedging" operations. For example, if a farmer knows he will have a large harvest of wheat to sell in six months, and his ability to make his mortgage payments and pay other expenses depends critically on the price of wheat, the farmer may want to "lock in" the price by selling futures contracts in wheat. On the other side of the transaction, a large operation that makes bread may itself want to lock in the price of one of its major inputs, so that a sudden price spike won't cripple operations. The bread producer would thus gladly *buy* the futures contracts issued by the farmer. This is a mutually beneficial arrangement in which no money changes hands in the present, but the two parties today lock in the price at which they will exchange wheat for money in the future. (Technically we have described a **forward contract**, which is economically very similar to a futures contract.) The use of futures contracts and other derivatives can allow market participants to hedge away their exposure to particular price swings, where they forfeit the potential benefits of a favorable move while avoiding the downside of an unfavorable move. This is the sense in which such contracts can serve as insurance.

- Mises warns (pp. 204–06) that a depreciating currency can lead to capital consumption. For a simple example, suppose a man spends $100,000 on a machine that lasts for ten years. If prices are stable (and disregarding interest), the man needs to earn at least $10,000 each year in sales revenue over and above labor and other expenses, in order to account for the depreciation on his machine. If inflation causes him to earn far more than he originally anticipated over the years from the sale of his goods, after setting aside $10,000 each year the man might spend the remaining "profit" on fancy dinners and vacation cruises. However, after ten years (with $100,000 in hand, disregarding interest) the man may discover that because of the fall in the purchasing power of money, a new machine has a price of $200,000. Thus the man unwittingly consumed half of his capital over the decade: he started with one new machine and ended up with the means to buy only half of a new machine. The man realizes that his fancy dinners and cruises were funded *not* out of profits but by eating away at his business assets.

## *New Terminology*

**Capital consumption:** A metaphor denoting the reduction in capital because of a failure to reinvest enough out of current output.

**Futures contract:** A standardized contract, traded on an organized exchange, where two parties agree to exchange a good at a specified price (the futures price) at a specified future date (the delivery date). As conditions change and alter the futures price pertaining to the delivery date, the exchange will credit or debit the accounts of the buyer and seller of the original futures contract on a daily basis to reflect the change. (If the futures price goes up, the buyer gains and the seller loses, etc.) These daily episodes of marking-to-market restore the market value of the futures contract itself to zero. Upon delivery, the seller of the futures contract delivers the good, while the buyer pays the current spot price for that date, *not* the futures price as originally specified.

**Forward contract:** Similar to a futures contract, though a forward contract is not standardized. Furthermore, there is no daily marking-to-market. On the delivery date, the buyer pays the forward price as originally specified in the contract. Thus the forward contract can achieve a positive or negative market value, as conditions change and cause the actual spot price (on the delivery date) to move above or below the originally specified forward price.

**Hedging transaction:** A financial transaction in which an individual attempts to reduce his or her exposure to a market outcome.

For example, someone who believes that Stock XYZ will outperform most other stocks might "go long" by purchasing several thousand shares of it. But to hedge himself against a general fall in the market, he might also "go short" an index fund holding all the stocks in the S&P 500. Thus, even if XYZ falls in price, the investor will still make money, so long as Stock XYZ drops by a smaller amount than most other stocks.

**Aleatory:** Dependent on chance, luck, or an uncertain outcome.

## *Study Questions*

1. Relate the following comment to Mises's earlier discussion (p. 61) of the hypothetical possibility of fiat money: "Lenders and borrowers are not in the habit of allowing for possible future fluctuations in the objective exchange value of money." (p. 195)

2. If the purchasing power of money *unexpectedly* falls, who is hurt—creditors or debtors? (p. 200)

3. What is necessary to eliminate the undesirable consequences of "unlimited inflationary policy"? (p. 203)

*4. Mises writes, "If the objective exchange value of all the stocks of money in the world could be instantaneously and in equal proportion increased or decreased, [and] if all at once the money-prices of all goods and services could rise or fall uniformly, the relative wealth of individual economic agents would not be affected" (p. 207). Does Mises's argument assume that everyone holds the same fraction of his or wealth in the form of cash balances, or does it also work if some people hold (say) large amounts of real estate, while others hold mostly cash? (Keep in mind that for this argument Mises has assumed away the problem of contracts for future goods.)

5. Explain: "Europe had exported ships and rails, metal goods and textiles, furniture and machines, for gold which it little needed or did not need at all, for what it had already was enough for all its monetary transactions." (p. 211)

---

*Questions with an asterisk signify the question is a particularly difficult one.

CHAPTER 13

# MONETARY POLICY

## *Summary*

Originally, citizens judged the success of monetary policy by the soundness of the coinage it maintained in circulation. In modern times **monetary policy** refers to government (or central bank) efforts to alter the purchasing power of money. The chief instrument through which the State carries out monetary policy is its strong influence on the *kind* of money used by the citizenry.

**Inflationism** is that monetary policy that seeks to increase the quantity of money. **Naïve inflationism** believes that money constitutes wealth, and that creating more money will turn poor into rich. A second group of inflationists understands that printing more money will cause prices to rise, but *endorses* the policy because they want to help debtors or achieve some other goal. A third group of inflationists understands that the policy in general will wreak economic havoc, but they support it too because they believe some essential government programs sometimes must be paid for through an "**inflation tax**." Economics can say, without making any value judgments, that inflationism is a very poor policy for achieving its stated objectives.

**Restrictionism** or **deflationism** is policy that aims at raising the objective exchange value of money. It is unpopular for various reasons.

Because neither inflationism nor deflationism is capable of achieving its stated objectives, the only sensible monetary policy is one that aims at eliminating all government interference with the purchasing power of money. In practice, this means a rigid adherence to a commodity standard, which in modern times means either the gold or silver standard.

In technical economic theory, the only coherent definition for **inflation** is an increase in the quantity of money (in the broader sense of the term) that is not offset by a corresponding increase in the demand for money (in the broader sense of the term), with the necessary result being a fall in the purchasing power of money. **Deflation** is the opposite, namely a reduction in the quantity of money that is not offset by a fall in the demand for it, such that prices tend to fall. The economist who wishes to influence public policy and avert disaster shouldn't lecture others on their sloppy use of terminology, but instead should expose the errors of *inflationism*.

## *Chapter Outline*

### 1. Monetary Policy Defined

Originally, citizens judged the success of monetary policy by the soundness of the coinage it maintained in circulation. If and when governments violated that trust by debasing the coinage, it was for fiscal (i.e., budgetary) ends: the authorities needed more money and so turned to inflation.

In modern times, however, governments use monetary policy to achieve other socio-political aims. Although particular factions may favor one monetary policy versus another because of the specific advantages they expect to derive—for example, the owners of gold mines favoring a return to the gold standard—in general **monetary policy** nowadays refers to government (or central bank) efforts to alter the purchasing power of money.

### 2. The Instruments of Monetary Policy

The chief instrument through which the State carries out monetary policy is its strong influence on the *kind* of money used by the citizenry. As controller of the mint and sole issuer of money substitutes, the modern State has wide discretion in this "choice" by its subjects. If the State decides to remain on a metallic standard (such as gold or silver), then it still must choose *which* precious metal. More generally, if the State opts for a credit or fiat money, then the State has the further option of altering the quantity of money at will, to achieve its objectives regarding the purchasing power of money.

## 3. Inflationism

**Inflationism** is that monetary policy that seeks to increase the quantity of money. **Naïve inflationism** believes that money constitutes wealth, and that creating more money will turn poor into rich. A second group of inflationists understands that printing more money will cause prices to rise (an elementary fact that the first group fails to see). Yet even so this second group *endorses* the policy, because they want to help debtors, or achieve some other goal, by raising prices. Finally, a third group of inflationists understands that the policy in general will wreak economic havoc, but they support it too because they believe some government programs (such as defense from foreign invaders) are absolutely essential, and sometimes must be paid for through an "**inflation tax**."

This third defense of inflation underscores the anti-democratic nature of the policy. Its proponents candidly admit that the public would never support certain programs (such as major wars) if they were forced to explicitly bear the full financial burden through taxation or government deficits financed by genuine savings. But when the programs are funded (partially) through the printing press, it is not clear to the average voter what is causing prices to rise and his standard of living to fall. He blames unions or currency speculators, not government spending.

Ironically, if the public anticipates a sharp *future* decline in the purchasing power of money because of an influx of new notes (printed by the government), then prices in the *present* can rise in expectation. Yet until the new notes physically exist, there may appear a shortage of notes. Thus the public and academics may clamor for more inflation, in order to satisfy the apparent "needs of commerce." Yet it is inflationism itself that has caused the problem, and further bouts will only exacerbate the situation.

Economic science cannot judge the policy objectives of inflationism; it cannot say whether it is proper to (say) help debtors or exporters at the expense of others. But what economics *can* say, without making any value judgments, is that inflationism is a very poor policy for achieving its stated objectives. Each of its alleged goals (helping debtors, helping exporters, etc.) can be achieved much more directly by other interventions besides a general debasement of the monetary unit. In this sense economics can criticize inflationism.

## 4. Restrictionism or Deflationism

**Restrictionism** or **deflationism** is policy that aims at raising the objective exchange value of money. It is unpopular for various reasons. First, governments do not benefit from it because they must sacrifice potential spending in order to (say) retire some of the notes collected through taxation. Second, a nation with an appreciating currency would see a "deteriorating" trade balance in the eyes of the public, which is also unpopular. Finally, the primary beneficiaries of deflationism are creditors, who generally speaking are a small and unpopular group.

The only time deflationism is politically viable occurs *after* a period of inflationism, either for matters of prestige or to assure international creditors to continue using a certain country's financial institutions. Yet even here, a policy of deflationism does not simply reverse the harms of the prior inflation, but instead causes many new harms of its own. For example, many of the creditors who will be helped by the current round of deflation were *not* the same people harmed during the inflation. In general it must be concluded that deflationism is a poor method for achieving the specific aims of its proponents.

## 5. Invariability of the Objective Exchange Value of Money as the Aim of Monetary Policy

If neither inflationism nor deflationism is capable of achieving its stated objectives, the only sensible monetary policy is one that aims at eliminating all government interference with the purchasing power of money. In practice, this means a rigid adherence to a commodity standard, which in modern times means either the gold or silver standard.

## 6. The Limits of Monetary Policy

As all government efforts to influence the purchasing power of money must ultimately work through the subjective valuations of individuals, in this realm as in others the government's power is limited. The authorities cannot anticipate the precise, long-run effects of their efforts to manipulate the currency, and this is one of the strongest arguments *against* such manipulation in the first place.

## 7. Excursus: The Concepts Inflation and Deflation

In technical economic theory, the only coherent definition for **inflation** is an increase in the quantity of money (in the broader sense of the term) that is not offset by a corresponding increase in the demand for money (in the broader sense of the term), with the necessary result being a fall in the purchasing power of money. **Deflation** is the opposite, namely a reduction in the quantity of money that is not offset by a fall in the demand for it, such that prices tend to fall. However, outside the realm of technical economics, the terms *inflation* and *deflation* have certain connotations. The economist who wishes to influence public policy and avert disaster shouldn't lecture others on their sloppy use of terminology, but instead should expose the errors of *inflationism*.

## *Technical Notes*

- On page 219 Mises writes, "If a country has a metallic standard, then the *only* measure of currency policy that it can carry out by itself is to go over to another kind of money." What Mises has in mind—and this is borne out by the important phrase "by itself"—is that the classical gold standard placed strict limits on each of the participating countries. In the period before the first World War, for example, the United States government pegged the dollar to 23.22 grains of gold (working out to around $20.67 per ounce), while the British government pegged its own currency at the rate of £4.25 to an ounce of gold. Thus the exchange rate between the dollar and British pound was fixed at $4.86 to a pound. If the United States government began printing up excessive amounts of new dollars, this would tend to cause domestic prices (quoted in dollars) to rise faster than they did (quoted in pounds) in Great Britain. Americans would start importing more from (cheaper) British producers, and the resulting trade deficit would allow the British to accumulate more and more dollars. This in turn would put pressure on the foreign exchange rate, which would (under a fiat standard) simply cause the dollar to depreciate against the British pound. But since both currencies were tied to gold at fixed rates, the falling dollar would open up an arbitrage opportunity for speculators to turn their dollars into the U.S. authorities in exchange for gold. Thus, as its gold reserves began to dwindle, the U.S. would have to abandon its inflationary path. Thus a metallic standard keeps sharp limits on the inflationary policies of any single country.

- On page 227 Mises writes, "In all countries where inflation has been rapid, it has been observed that the decrease in the value of the money has occurred faster than the increase in its quantity." On the following page he explains that the value of money is influenced by both supply *and* demand. For a modern example, suppose that the Chairman of the Federal Reserve announced that he would cause the quantity of U.S. dollars to rise by a factor of 1,000 in the course of a week. Even ignoring the step-by-step process of inflation, the end result would *not* simply be a general 1,000-fold rise in prices. Instead, prices (quoted in U.S. dollars) would rise by much *more* than that, because Americans would no longer want to hold dollars. They would no longer view the dollar as a safe currency, and would seek to replace their dollar holdings with either other currencies or perhaps the precious metals. In order to restore equilibrium, then, prices would have to rise not merely on account of the extra quantity of dollars, but also because of the sharp drop in the subjective desire to hold them.

## *New Terminology*

**Monetary policy:** Government or central bank efforts to alter the purchasing power of money.

**Inflationism:** Monetary policy that seeks to increase the quantity of money.

**Naïve inflationism:** Inflationism supported by the belief that money constitutes wealth.

**Inflation tax:** The redistribution of wealth from the citizenry to the government (or its designated beneficiaries) through inflation.

**Restrictionism/Deflationism:** Monetary policy that aims at raising the objective exchange value of money.

**Inflation:** An increase in the quantity of money (in the broader sense of the term) that is not offset by a corresponding increase in the demand for money (in the broader sense of the term), with the necessary result being a fall in the purchasing power of money. (Note that this is a technical economic definition, not necessarily having the connotations of "inflation" in popular discussions.)

**Deflation:** A reduction in the quantity of money that is not offset by a fall in the demand for it, such that prices tend to fall. (Note that this is a technical economic definition, not necessarily having the connotations of "deflation" in popular discussions.)

## *Study Questions*

1. What unflattering possibility does Mises suggest regarding Ben Franklin's support of paper money early in his career? (p. 217)

2. Why does "naïve inflationism" recommend an increase in the quantity of money? (pp. 219–20)

3. Is it possible for someone to support inflationism, even if he understands that it will have grave economic consequences? (pp. 221–22)

4. Explain: "[I]nflation becomes the most important psychological resource of any economic policy whose consequences have to be concealed; and so in this sense it can be called an instrument of *unpopular*, i.e., of anti-democratic, policy, since by misleading public opinion it makes possible the continued existence of a system of government that would have no hope of the consent of the people if the circumstances were clearly laid before them." (pp. 223–24)

5. Would Mises have been surprised by the second half of the twentieth century, since he writes, "In the long run, a money which continually fell in value would have no commercial utility. It could not be used as a standard of deferred payments" (p. 227)?

CHAPTER 14

# THE MONETARY POLICY OF ÉTATISM

## *Summary*

**Étatism** as a theory is the doctrine of the omnipotence of the State. As a policy, étatism is the attempt to regulate all social and economic affairs by authoritative commandment and prohibition.

The étatist views money as a creature of the State, and hence (erroneously) believes that a powerful and rich State should have a correspondingly "good" money. But history is full of cases where even the victors in a war saw the collapse of their currency, or where a wealthy country had a very weak currency.

Often the authorities will try to mitigate the consequences of inflationism by imposing price controls. If the controls are applied to a small number of items, then **shortages** will develop because the producers of these items will see other prices rise but will not be able to charge appropriate prices for the items in question. The authorities must then either abandon their policy or intervene further still, controlling more prices and possibly compelling people to work against their will.

A popular view holds that a country experiencing a **debit balance of payments** cannot stabilize the value of its money, until the underlying defects are rectified. However, if a country uses purely metallic money, then a debit balance of payments will eventually reverse itself automatically, because the outflow of metal will lead to falling domestic prices. For countries on credit or fiat money, a similar principle holds. A debit balance of payments per se cannot unilaterally cause a nation's currency to depreciate, because the debit balance itself is caused by inflation. No matter the foreign trade situation, a country can always choose sound money.

If the government wishes to avoid having its currency "attacked" by speculators, it need only abandon inflationist policies.

## *Chapter Outline*

### 1. The Monetary Theory of Étatism

**Étatism** as a theory is the doctrine of the omnipotence of the State. As a policy, étatism is the attempt to regulate all social and economic affairs by authoritative commandment and prohibition. Although the outward appearances of private property and entrepreneurship may be left intact, in practice étatism can only be realized as State Socialism. Because sociology and economics detail the limits on what sheer might can achieve in attempting to redesign human society, étatists seek to discredit these fields.

### 2. National Prestige and the Rate of Exchange

The étatist views money as a creature of the State, and hence (erroneously) believes that a powerful and rich State should have a correspondingly "good" money (i.e., money with a high exchange rate). But history is full of cases where even the victors in a war saw the collapse of their currency, or where a wealthy country had a very weak currency.

### 3. The Regulation of Prices by Authoritative Decree

Often the authorities will try to mitigate the consequences of inflationism by imposing price controls, in which people are punished by fines or prison sentences for asking (or even paying) prices above the legal ceiling. If the controls are applied to a small number of items, then **shortages** will develop because the producers of these items will see other prices rise but will not be able to charge appropriate prices for the items in question. This outcome is the opposite of what the authorities intended; they had imposed the price controls to keep the items accessible to the public, not to eradicate them from the store shelves. At this point, the authorities must either abandon their policy or intervene further still, controlling more prices and possibly compelling people to work against their will.

## 4. The Balance-of-Payments Theory as a Basis of Currency Policy

A popular view holds that a country experiencing a **debit balance of payments** cannot stabilize the value of its money, until the underlying defects are rectified. However, the classical economists and later the Currency School demonstrated the flaws in this view. If a country uses purely metallic money, then a debit balance of payments will eventually reverse itself automatically, because the outflow of metal (such as gold) will lead to falling domestic prices. Eventually, residents will prefer to buy from domestic producers rather than foreigners, and foreign purchasers will prefer to buy more cheaply from them as well. Thus the debit balance will turn into a **credit balance of payments**, and the monetary metal will tend to flow back into the country that originally experienced the drain.

For countries on credit or fiat money, a similar principle holds. A debit balance of payments per se cannot unilaterally cause a nation's currency to depreciate, because the debit balance itself is caused by inflation. No matter the foreign trade situation, a country can always choose sound money.

## 5. The Suppression of Speculation

When inflationist policies lead to a depreciation of a country's money against other currencies, government officials will often denounce foreign speculators for "attacking the currency." Yet in general, speculators cannot alter the average price of a good (including money), they simply smooth out the ups and downs. The speculator tries to buy low and sell high (or vice versa). By buying undervalued currencies, the speculator pushes *up* the price toward its long-run level, and by selling overvalued currencies, the speculator pushes them down toward the "correct" level. If the government wishes to avoid having its currency "attacked" by speculators, it need only abandon inflationist policies.

## *Important Contributions*

- On pages 246–48, Mises explains the process by which limited interventions lead to undesirable consequences, even from the point of view of the authorities. These in turn lead to further interventions, in an attempt to counteract the bad consequences. The process continues until the authorities either abandon their program or reach full-blown socialism. Although economists before Mises understood the undesirable effects of price ceilings, this broader dynamic was something that Mises stressed throughout his career. Mises contrasted the virtues of a free market versus outright socialism, precisely because he thought it was a mirage to endorse a "**mixed economy**" that avoided either extreme. In fact in 1950 he would deliver a speech entitled, "Middle of the Road Policy Leads to Socialism."

- On pages 249–52, Mises showcases his numerous talents as an economist. He demonstrates a command of pure economic theory, the history of economic thought, and the day-to-day activities in the actual foreign exchange market. It is only because of his mastery of all three areas that he can so confidently explain the errors in rival doctrines, and why the businessman is fooled by correlations that do not represent actual causality when it comes to trade flows and exchange rates.

## *New Terminology*

**Étatism (as theory):** The doctrine of the omnipotence of the State.

**Étatism (as policy):** The attempt to regulate all social and economic affairs by authoritative commandment and prohibition.

**Mixed economy:** An economy possessing aspects of both capitalism and socialism, in which private individuals retain nominal ownership of the means of production, but the government extensively regulates their use of this property, including wages, interest rates, and other prices set on the market.

**Debit balance of payments:** The situation occurring when the people of a country collectively spend more on foreign goods and assets than vice versa. It is settled by an outflow of money from the country.

**Credit balance of payments:** The situation occurring when the people of a country collectively spend less on foreign goods and assets than vice versa. It is settled by an inflow of money to the country.

**Shortages:** A shortfall in the quantity of goods offered for sale, compared to the amount consumers wish to purchase. Shortages are caused when a price ceiling holds the price below the market-clearing level.

## *Study Questions*

1. Why does economic science pose a threat to étatism? (p. 243)

2. After a price ceiling is imposed, what happens once the stocks of goods that were already on the shelves have been sold off? (p. 247)

3. Explain: "If the regulation of prices had been successful, it would have paralyzed the whole economic organism. The only thing that made possible the continued functioning of the social apparatus of production was the incomplete enforcement of the regulations that was due to the paralysis of the efforts of those who ought to have executed them." (p. 248)

4. Explain: "Price fluctuations are reduced by speculation, not aggravated, as the popular legend has it." (p. 253)

5. Explain: "The fluctuations of the foreign-exchange rate are not determined solely by bears selling but just as much by bulls buying." (p. 253)

PART III

# MONEY AND BANKING

CHAPTER 15

# THE BUSINESS OF BANKING

## *Summary*

A **banker** is one who lends out other people's money; a **capitalist** lends out his or her own money. The business of banking falls into two distinct categories: (1) the negotiation of credit through the loan of other people's money and (2) the granting of credit through the issue of fiduciary media.

In their role as negotiator of credit (or **credit intermediaries**), banks borrow from lenders at a certain rate of interest and then lend it to borrowers at (what promises to be) a higher rate of interest.

Credit transactions involve the exchange of present for future goods. Credit transactions can be divided into two groups: (1) Those in which one party has the benefit of obtaining a good in the present while the other party has the disadvantage of providing a good in the present, and (2) those in which one party has the benefit of obtaining a good in the present while the other party does *not* suffer any corresponding disadvantage. Loans of the first type (in which the lender actually renounces the use of his money) involve **commodity credit** while loans of the second type (in which the bank issues fiduciary media) involve **circulation credit**.

The crucial feature in loans of fiduciary media is that the original depositor is *not* engaged in a credit transaction. He retains the full use of his money, even as the bank lends it to someone else.

This process increases the total amount of money in the broader sense.

Only by recognizing the fundamental distinction between notes and **current accounts** that are either (*a*) backed versus (*b*) unbacked by money, can the economist hope to understand the broader role that fiduciary media play in economic cycles.

## *Chapter Outline*

### 1. Types of Banking Activity

A **banker** is one who lends out other people's money; a **capitalist** lends out his or her own money. The business of banking falls into two distinct categories: (1) the negotiation of credit through the loan of other people's money and (2) the granting of credit through the issue of fiduciary media. (Recall that fiduciary media are notes and bank balances—claims on money—that are not actually covered by money in reserve.)

### 2. The Banks as Negotiators of Credit

In their role as negotiator of credit (or **credit intermediaries**), banks borrow from lenders at a certain rate of interest and then lend it to borrowers at (what promises to be) a higher rate of interest. In this activity, prudent banks will obey the **golden rule** by which their liabilities will not mature earlier than their assets. In other words, the banks should *not* "borrow short to lend long," if they want to avoid the risk of insolvency. Following the golden rule, by matching the maturities of assets and liabilities, will not eliminate all risks of course, because any investment could go sour and the borrower default on the loan from the bank.

### 3. The Banks as Issuers of Fiduciary Media

Credit transactions involve the exchange of present for future goods. Credit transactions can be divided into two groups: (1) Those in which one party has the benefit of obtaining a good in the present while the other party has the disadvantage of providing a good in the present, and (2) those in which one party has the benefit of obtaining a good in the present while the other party does *not* suffer any corresponding disadvantage. This second class of credit transactions is possible when a creditor issues fiduciary media; this person lends without really giving anything up. Loans of the first type (in which the lender actually renounces the use of his money) involve **commodity credit** while loans of fiduciary media involve **circulation credit**.

For all goods, an absolutely secure and immediately redeemable claim will inherit the market value of the good itself. However, what makes fiduciary media special is that they can *indefinitely* function as money substitutes, since (unlike all other goods) nobody ever is the final "consumer" of money proper. Therefore, claims to it can circulate in the community without ever being redeemed, which allows the banks to issue fiduciary media in the first place.

## 4. Deposits as the Origin of Circulation Credit

The issue of fiduciary media is intimately connected with the deposit system. A customer will deposit actual money with the bank, which then is the basis upon which fiduciary media (i.e., unbacked claims to money) are issued. The crucial feature in these operations is that economically speaking, the original depositor is *not* engaged in a credit transaction. He is not lending the bank his money, but is merely depositing it, because he still retains the full economic use of his money in the present. Therefore by granting new loans *on top* of such deposits, the banks increase the total amount of money in the broader sense. They are not mere credit intermediaries, but instead are granting the economic use of money to a new group, without taking it away from the original group.

## 5. The Granting of Circulation Credit

The specific method of issuance of fiduciary media is irrelevant for its effects on the value of money. The bank might (1) literally lend out the original depositor's money (while the original depositor still believes he has full and immediate claim to it), (2) issue other bank clients banknotes which may be redeemed with the depositor's money, or (3) grant new loans in the form of checkbook accounts, with the depositor's money serving as part of the reserves behind the new loan. [NOTE: A full description of the accounting of fractional-reserve banking is available in the lecture, "The Theory of Central Banking," at: http://www.youtube.com/watch?v=6HAEPSt_12U]

Some writers treat the expansion of banks' note-issue as akin to an increase in the community's demand for credit. But if the community tries to borrow more, perhaps by issuing more **bills of exchange**, then the interest rate tends to go up. In contrast, the bank *supplies* credit: when it issues more notes, the rate of interest (at least initially) goes down.

## 6. Fiduciary Media and the Nature of Indirect Exchange

Only by recognizing the fundamental distinction between notes and **current accounts** that are either (*a*) backed versus (*b*) unbacked by money, can the economist hope to understand the broader role that fiduciary media play in economic cycles. On the other hand, it is also a mistake to deny fiduciary media's ability to facilitate indirect exchanges. When someone sells a commodity for a banknote, and then uses the banknote to purchase another commodity, this is an indirect exchange just as surely as if the person had used money proper.

## *Important Contributions*

- In the beginning of this chapter, Mises divides banking into two categories: the negotiation of credit through the loan of other people's money, and the issue of fiduciary media. (Murray Rothbard, in his work on banking, classifies the two activities as **loan banking** versus **deposit banking**.) Although other writers are familiar with these concepts, Mises shone a spotlight on the distinction and will go on to point out the problems with the issue of fiduciary media (i.e., deposit banking) that some earlier economists had discovered.

- Continuing with the previous note, Mises explains his settling on the terms commodity credit and circulation credit on pages 264–65. Precisely because he believes the issuance of fiduciary media play such a crucial role in the boom-bust cycle in market economies, Mises is designing his theoretical edifice to highlight the phenomenon.

## *New Terminology*

**Banker:** A person who lends out other people's money.

**Capitalist:** A person who lends out his or her own money.

**Credit intermediaries:** Institutions that act as "middlemen" between lenders and borrowers.

**Golden rule (of bank lending):** Matching the maturities of assets and liabilities, so that the bank is not dependent on the ability to "roll over" maturing debt. If a bank does not follow the golden rule, increases in short-term interest rates can lead to disaster, when the bank must pay its own creditors while its assets are not yet due.

**Commodity Credit:** A loan granted through the renunciation of the use of present goods by the lender. Commodity credit may involve money certificates but not fiduciary media.

**Circulation Credit:** A loan granted even though the lender does *not* sacrifice the use of present goods. Circulation credit involves the use of fiduciary media.

**Bill of exchange:** A non-interest-bearing written order that binds one party to a pay a fixed sum of money to another party at a specified future date or upon demand. A bill of exchange is generally transferable through endorsement.

**Current accounts (in banking):** Accounts held with a bank, giving the owner the ability to write drafts or withdraw money upon demand. (Today a standard "checking account" would be an example.)

**Loan banking:** Banking through the use of commodity credit, where the bank receives loans from one group of savers in order to itself make loans to another group of borrowers. The savers do not consider this money as part of their cash balances during the term of the loan to the bank.

**Deposit banking:** Banking through the use of circulation credit, where the bank receives deposits into current accounts from one group of clients in order to make loans to another group of borrowers. The depositors consider this money to be part of their cash balances, even though much of it has been lent out to others.

## *Study Questions*

1. Does Mises realize that modern banks perform other operations besides the two types of banking he mentions? (pp. 261–62)

2. Explain: "A person who has a thousand loaves of bread at his immediate disposal will not dare to issue more than a thousand tickets each of which gives its holder the right to demand at any time the delivery of a loaf of bread. It is otherwise with money." (p. 267)

3. Why does Mises say that fiduciary media "can therefore be created only by banks and bankers"? (p. 269)

4. How does the issue of fiduciary media affect the objective exchange value of money? (p. 268)

5. Explain: "[Credit circulation] loans are granted out of a fund *that did not exist before the loans were granted.*" (p. 271)

CHAPTER 16

# THE EVOLUTION OF FIDUCIARY MEDIA

## *Chapter Outline*

### 1. The Two Ways of Issuing Fiduciary Media

Fiduciary media may be issued by banks or by non-banks (primarily the government). Banks can issue fiduciary media either through banknotes or by granting deposits in a current account (i.e., a modern-day checking account). Banks treat their outstanding fiduciary media as liabilities on their balance sheets, and must loan or directly invest them wisely.

Governments may also issue fiduciary media such as **convertible Treasury notes** and token coins. Governments often do not set aside a credit fund out of their capital to "cover" the increased obligations. Instead governments will pocket the **seigniorage** as income just as surely as tax revenue.

### 2. Fiduciary Media and the Clearing System

The use of fiduciary media can reduce the demand for money in the narrower sense. For example, in the modern United States, the demand to hold actual Federal Reserve notes (green pieces of paper with pictures of dead presidents) is much lower, because people can open checking accounts with commercial banks and write checks or use debit cards (where these deposits are partly fiduciary media, because they are not fully backed up by cash in the vault).

However, an entirely different phenomenon is the reduction in the demand for money in the broader sense—including money proper and even money substitutes (including fiduciary media)—brought about by the development of **credit** and the clearing system. If one party to a transaction is willing to defer receiving payment, he has thus granted credit. If the other party later delivers goods or performs services such that the original debt is partially or fully offset, only the difference needs to be settled by actual money or money substitutes. As more such transactions are incorporated into such arrangements, the community's demand for money in the broader sense falls below what it otherwise would have been.

## 3. Fiduciary Media in Domestic Trade

So long as a country has a stable legal framework that permits the building of trust in issuers, the use of clearing operations and fiduciary media can grow to dominate transactions and almost completely displace the use of money in the narrower sense.

## 4. Fiduciary Media in International Trade

The practice of using claims and counter-claims in clearing operations to reduce the need to transport money was of particular benefit in international trade, because of the longer distances and time involved. However, fiduciary media themselves are still limited by national boundaries. For example, a particular supplier in the United States might grant credit to a merchant in France, but the claim on the French merchant would not circulate from hand to hand in the same way that a banknote in the United States (or in France) could. Only with the development of a world bank, with clientele drawn from every country, could fiduciary media transcend national boundaries.

## Technical Notes

- On page 278 Mises writes, "[Bank fiduciary media] are entered as liabilities, and the issuing body does not regard the sum issued as an increase of its income or capital, but as an increase on the debit side of its account, which must be balanced by a corresponding increase on the credit side if the whole transaction is not to figure as a loss. This way of dealing with fiduciary media makes it necessary for the issuing body to regard them as part of its trading capital and never to spend them on consumption but always to invest them in business." This is a crucial point that newcomers to fractional-reserve banking often miss. Even though such bankers in a sense "create money out of thin air," they can't simply open up a new account for $100,000 and then write checks to buy themselves sports cars and designer clothes. The reason is that the merchants in the community would then have $100,000 in claims on the actual cash reserves of the bank, and ultimately the bank's vault would run out of the genuine money. What fractional bankers do instead is *loan* out the $100,000 to a productive business at (say) 5 percent interest. When the $105,000 is repaid in a year, the $100,000 that was initially created can be "destroyed" (through bookkeeping) and the $5,000 in interest income can be safely spent without draining the bank's cash reserves. Thus fractional-reserve bankers create money out of thin air *not* to directly spend it—which would be incredibly reckless and short-lived—but instead to *earn interest income* from it.

- On page 291 Mises rejects the claim that India and other Asiatic countries used gold as a "measure of prices" while retaining silver as a medium of exchange. For one thing, the modern subjective value theory explodes the very notion of money as a measure, since value is not an objective property like length or weight that can be measured. Yet of more relevance to this passage, Mises is pointing out that even in the classical gold standard countries, people rarely used actual gold when buying goods and services. Instead, they employed *claims* to gold. But this is precisely what happened in India, which retained silver coins in circulation that could be redeemed for the official money, gold, at a certain exchange rate.

## *New Terminology*

**Convertible Treasury notes:** Paper notes issued by the government that entitle the bearer to redemption in money upon demand.

**Seigniorage:** The difference between the market value of money and the cost to produce it.

**Credit:** The ability to receive present goods in exchange for the promise of delivering (typically a greater number of) future goods.

## *Study Questions*

1. Explain: "To complete [a] transaction ... by full or partial cancellation of counter-claims offers important advantages in comparison with direct exchange: all the freedom connected with the use of money is combined with the technical simplicity that characterizes direct exchange transactions." (p. 282)

2. What does Mises think is the importance of credit for the monetary system? (p. 282)

3. Explain: "Money in these cases [of international clearing operations] is still a medium of exchange, but its employment in this capacity is independent of its physical existence. Use is made of money, but not *physical* use of actually existing money or money substitutes. Money which is not present performs an economic function; it has its effect solely by reason of the possibility of its being *able* to be present." (p. 283)

4. Does Mises classify bills of exchange as fiduciary media? (pp. 285–86)

5. If a hypothetical world bank had deposits and notes that were backed up 100 percent by money on reserve, could it economize on money payments? (p. 294)

CHAPTER 17

# FIDUCIARY MEDIA AND THE DEMAND FOR MONEY

## *Summary*


If labor and other resources are used to extract more gold from mines, and this additional gold goes into the cash balances of people in the community, then from a social point of view the labor and other resources have been wasted. The quantity of "real output" (pounds of steak, barrels of crude oil, etc.) produced per person doesn't rise, but merely the *prices* of these items quoted in gold or silver.

The development of fiduciary media kept the objective exchange value of money lower than it otherwise would have been, and thereby avoided a large diversion of resources into mining more of the precious metals for cash holdings.

Some writers argue that the payment system in an advanced market economy is "elastic" and responds to the "needs of commerce," rather than the actual stock of money in the narrower sense. Although the extension of the clearing system *does* reduce the demand for money in the broader sense, there is no reason that its development should be related to the demand for money. It is an independent phenomenon that may either strengthen or counterbalance changes in the demand for money originating from other causes.

Many writers (such as those of the **Banking School**) argue that the banks do not have the power to independently increase the quantity of fiduciary media. What these writers fail to understand is that the demand for loans depends on the rate of interest. It makes no sense to speak of how much money the banks' customers wish to borrow, without specifying a rate of interest. If the banks want to issue fiduciary media, they must lower the market rate below the **natural rate of interest**.

Businesses seek loans from the banks because they desire capital; they simply want capital *in the form of money*, so that they can conveniently acquire the physical capital goods that they ultimately desire for their operations. Of course, the mere issuance of fiduciary media does not increase the amount of tractors, fertilizer, or power tools. The only way the banks can provide these goods to their clients is through redistribution of purchasing power away from members of the community who do not receive the influx of the newly created money.

## *Chapter Outline*

### 1. The Influence of Fiduciary Media on the Demand for Money in the Narrower Sense

In one sense, the employment of the precious metals (or any other useful commodity) to enlarge the stock of money is wasteful. If labor and other resources are used to extract more gold from mines, and this additional gold goes *not* into industrial or commercial uses (such as for dental fillings or jewelry), but instead increases the cash balances of people in the community, then from a social point of view the labor and other resources have been wasted. Increasing the quantity of money may redistribute existing wealth to make some individuals richer, but only at the expense of making others (who are last to receive the new money) poorer. The community as a whole doesn't achieve a higher standard of living, simply because people hold more gold or silver in their cash balances. The quantity of "real output" (pounds of steak, barrels of crude oil, etc.) produced per person doesn't rise, but merely the *prices* of these items quoted in gold or silver.

The development of fiduciary media reduces the demand to hold money in the narrower sense. In a community using gold as commodity money, a person who holds (airtight and instantly redeemable) claims to gold, which are accepted in commerce by everyone in the community, doesn't need to carry as much *actual* gold on a day-to-day basis. In this sense the widespread use of fiduciary media "economizes" on the amount of metal that must be allocated into the function of serving as the medium of exchange; more gold is freed up to be used in jewelry or industrial applications.

Were it not for the simultaneous development of fiduciary media, the intensification of the division of labor as the world became one giant integrated market would have led to a sharp increase in the objective exchange value of money. In other words, as more people around the world became part of the global market which used gold as the international money, more people would have tried to obtain gold as part of their cash holdings. If actual gold had to satisfy this huge growth in demand, prices (quoted in gold) would have fallen and the owners of gold mines would have intensified their extraction efforts. But the simultaneous development of fiduciary media counterbalanced this tendency, so that the purchasing power of a unit of gold did not rise as much as it otherwise would have.

## 2. The Fluctuations in the Demand for Money

Some of the fluctuations in the demand for money are quite predictable. An increase in population and the spread of the money economy increase the demand for money. The demand for money changes during boom and bust periods. And even in a typical year, there are cyclical patterns based on agriculture and the payment of workers.

## 3. The Elasticity of the System of Reciprocal Cancellation

Some writers argue that the payment system in an advanced market economy is "elastic" and responds to the "needs of commerce," rather than the actual stock of money in the narrower sense. The quantity of money is said to have little influence on the objective exchange value of money, because (say) an increase in the demand for money will automatically be counterbalanced by other forces. These claims are often difficult to evaluate because they fail to make the crucial distinction between the extension of the clearing system, versus the increased use of fiduciary media. Although the extension of the clearing system *does* reduce the demand for money in the broader sense, there is no reason that its development should be related to the demand for money. It is an independent phenomenon that may either strengthen or counterbalance changes in the demand for money originating from other causes.

## 4. The Elasticity of a Credit Circulation Based on Bills, Especially on Commodity Bills

Many writers (such as those of the **Banking School**) argue that the banks do not have the power to independently increase the quantity of fiduciary media. If business needs require more transactions, then somehow or other, business will get it—either from banks issuing more fiduciary media, or from businesses developing techniques to economize on the use of money. On the other hand (so the argument continues), if the banks try to issue more fiduciary media than the business community desires, these excess notes will come flowing back to the banks.

What these writers fail to understand is that the demand for loans depends on the rate of interest. It makes no sense to speak of how much money the banks' customers wish to borrow, without specifying a rate of interest. If the banks want to issue fiduciary media, they must lower the market rate below the **natural rate of interest**.

## 5. The Significance of the Exclusive Employment of Bills as Cover for Fiduciary Media

The German Bank Act of 1875 followed the famous **Peel's Act** in imposing requirements on the **cover** that banks could accept when issuing new loans in excess of their gold deposits. The requirement was significant *not* because it somehow tied the expansion of credit to the desire of the community for more money. Rather, it was significant because it placed an obstacle in the issuance of fiduciary media, keeping the quantity of money in the broader sense lower than it otherwise would have been.

## 6. The Periodical Rise and Fall in the Extent to Which Bank Credit is Requisitioned

Businesses seek loans from the banks because they desire capital; they simply want capital *in the form of money*, so that they can conveniently acquire the physical capital goods that they ultimately desire for their operations. Of course, the mere issuance of fiduciary media does not increase the amount of tractors, fertilizer, or power tools. The only way the banks can provide these goods to their clients is through redistribution of purchasing power away from members of the community who do not receive the influx of the newly created money.

## 7. The Influence of Fiduciary Media on Fluctuations in the Objective Exchange Value of Money

As with the extension of clearing operations, there is no reason that the expansion or contraction of fiduciary media should mirror changes in the demand to hold money; there is no "automatic" mechanism by which the objective exchange value of money is stabilized. Thus the insights of the quantity theory are upheld.

## *Technical Notes*

- An example will clarify the terminology and arguments running throughout this and earlier chapters. Suppose a man asks his bartender if he can "run a tab," meaning that he will obtain drinks in the present but will pay money for them later (perhaps at the end of the month). The bartender agrees, saying the man can have up to $100 in drinks without having to pay for them upfront. By doing so, the bartender has extended *credit* to the man. However, the quantity of *money* in the man's possession hasn't increased, because the man doesn't have any transferrable claim (issued by the bartender) that others in the community would accept. In contrast, if the man goes to his local bank and applies for a $100 loan (to be paid back at the end of the month), then in this case too the man receives an extension of credit, but he *also* receives an addition to his cash balances. Whether the bank loan consists of a new checking account (with $100 as the initial balance), actual money, or notes issued by the bank, these would all be classified as money in the broader sense. The man could use them to buy anything he wanted, including drinks at the bar. Finally, to see the limited role of clearing systems, revert to the original assumption, where the man's credit consists of a "tab" issued by the bartender with a limit of $100. If the man wanted to use this credit *not* to buy alcoholic drinks, but rather to buy (say) a pair of shoes, he would have to find a shoe seller who also wanted to buy drinks from the particular bar in question. Then it might be possible to arrange a deal whereby the man acquires the shoes, in exchange for telling the bartender to put the shoe seller's drinks on his own tab (rather than charging the shoe seller for them).

- Mises concludes his discussion of section 4 on page 312 by saying, "[A]ll of this is true only under the assumption that all banks issue fiduciary media according to uniform principles, or that there is only one bank that issues fiduciary media." In the section, Mises had criticized the writers of the Banking School who argued that the banks couldn't get the community to accept extra issues of fiduciary media, if the community didn't want to hold them. Mises objected that the demand for the additional loans could be influenced by the rate of interest the banks charged, and hence the Banking School's views were mistaken. So long as they are willing to sufficiently lower the rate of interest below the natural rate, the banks can convince the community to accept any amount of new fiduciary media. However, Mises does *not* mean that an individual bank has no checks on its issue. If any single bank unilaterally lowers its interest rate and issues more fiduciary media (compared to the policies of its competitors), then eventually those notes will fall into the hands of people who are not clients of the expanding bank. When these people deposit the bank's newly issued notes with their own banks (which are competitors), these notes will be presented for redemption in money in the narrower sense. Thus the lone bank engaged in an expansionary policy will soon see its reserves of money proper dwindle, and will have to abandon its experiment. Yet this mechanism is not what the Banking School theorists had in mind when they said banks couldn't issue more notes than the needs of the community warranted.

## *New Terminology*

**Banking School:** An English school of thought which argued that the banks were incapable of independently altering the rate of interest or the purchasing power of money, because the market would use clearing operations, bills of exchange, and other techniques to receive the credit it demanded for business purposes.

**Currency School:** An English school of thought which argued that the banks caused economic crises through the expansion and contraction of credit. However, the Currency School thought the suppression of the issue of fiduciary media in the form of banknotes (which was codified in Peel's Act) would solve the problem, because its members erroneously excluded demand (or current account) deposits from their analysis.

**(Wicksellian) natural rate of interest:** Developed by economist Knut Wicksell, the hypothetical rate of interest that would occur if goods were traded directly against each other without the use of money.

**Peel's Act [Bank Charter Act 1844]:** An important legislative act that took the power of issuing new notes away from private banks and vested it completely with the Bank of England, which itself was required to maintain 100 percent metallic backing for any new notes that it issued. However, the Act crucially did *not* impose such a restriction on the extension of deposits, meaning that private banks could create more fiduciary media by granting loans (not backed by gold) to their customers.

**Cover (of note issue):** Assets backing the issue of new banknotes. Depending on the regulations, a bank might issue fiduciary media not backed by money itself, but backed by another asset such as a commodity bill.

**Working capital:** Current assets minus current liabilities. More generally, a measure of a firm's ability to quickly turn some of its assets into cash in order to finance an expansion.

**Fixed capital:** Assets embodied in durable investments such as factories and specialized equipment that will be used over a long period.

## *Study Questions*

1. What was Adam Smith's analogy to explain the drawback of using the precious metals as money? (p. 298)

2. If fiat or credit money is employed, does it still make sense to use fiduciary media to economize on the use of money in the narrower sense? (pp. 299–300)

3. Why would population growth influence the demand to hold money? (pp. 300–01)

4. Explain: "The demand for money and money substitutes that is expressed on the loan market is in the last resort a demand for capital goods or, when consumption credit is involved, for consumption goods." (p. 307)

5. Who bears the "cost of creating capital for borrowers of loans granted in fiduciary media"? (p. 314)

CHAPTER 18

# THE REDEMPTION OF FIDUCIARY MEDIA

## *Summary*

The confidence in a bank's ability to redeem its fiduciary media is an all-or-nothing proposition: if a portion of the community panics and rushes to redeem their claims, then *everyone* does. By their very nature, fiduciary media cannot all be honored by the bank at once. Consequently, some writers suggest an outright prohibition on the practice. However, historically this requirement would have led to a much larger diversion of resources into the production of the precious metals as the demand for money increased.

A bank operating in a competitive environment can only issue as much fiduciary media as its own customers wish to hold, for transactions among themselves. Whenever a bank's customer seeks to do business with someone outside the clientele of the bank, the customer must convert his claims into money in the narrower sense, because the other person will not wish to accept the bank's promises to pay.

**Solvency** means that an institution (such as a bank) could shut down, sell off all of its assets, and raise at least enough money to pay off all of its creditors. **Liquidity** is a stronger condition, meaning that the institution's assets deliver a **cash flow** allowing it to pay its liabilities *on time*. If a firm is liquid, it is solvent, but it might be solvent while illiquid. Banks issuing fiduciary media are always illiquid.

Sometimes legislation, but always public opinion, compels the banks to give preference to short-term rather than long-term loans. This is a quite valid preference, backed up by centuries of experience, simply because it limits a bank's ability to issue fiduciary media.

## *Chapter Outline*

### 1. The Necessity for Complete Equivalence Between Money and Money Substitutes

So long as some people believe that a claim to money issued by a particular institution is absolutely reliable and can be redeemed upon demand, these people may pass such claims among themselves as if they were money. This is what makes them money substitutes. However, the issuing institution must always keep a reserve fund of money in the narrower sense to redeem the claims whenever they are presented, in order to maintain this trust. Such redemptions will be requested whenever the bank's own clientele wish to use their claims to do business with someone outside the clientele, i.e., a person who does *not* consider the claim to be a substitute for money in the narrower sense.

### 2. The Return of Fiduciary Media to the Issuer on Account of Lack of Confidence on the Part of the Holders

The confidence in a bank's ability to redeem its fiduciary media is an all-or-nothing proposition: if a portion of the community panics and rushes to redeem their claims, then *everyone* does. By their very nature, fiduciary media cannot all be honored by the bank at once. No matter how wisely a bank manages its assets, it will not be able to pay out money in the narrower sense for all of its outstanding claims, if customers show up en masse and demand redemption—assuming the bank has been issuing fiduciary media.

## 3. The Case Against the Issue of Fiduciary Media

Because of the internal contradiction of the nature of fiduciary media—which renders every issuing institution liable to ruin—some writers suggest an outright prohibition on the practice. However, historically this requirement would have led to a much larger diversion of resources into the production of the precious metals as the demand for money increased. The banks could survive even if they were legally required to maintain 100 percent reserves covering all note issues and deposits; it is not consideration for the practice of banking that led legislators to tolerate fiduciary media. Rather, it was the desire to avoid a large increase in the objective exchange value of money (i.e., a general fall in prices of goods and services).

## 4. The Redemption Fund

A bank operating in a competitive environment—where its rivals may pursue different policies and where its own clientele is only a fraction of the whole community using the same money—can only issue as much fiduciary media as its own customers wish to hold, for transactions among themselves. Whenever a bank's customer seeks to do business with someone outside the clientele of the bank, the customer must convert his claims (whether in the form of notes or a checkbook deposit) into money in the narrower sense, because the other person will not wish to accept the bank's promises to pay.

## 5. The So-called "Banking" Type of Cover for Fiduciary Media

**Solvency** means that an institution (such as a bank) could shut down, sell off all of its assets, and raise at least enough money to pay off all of its creditors. **Liquidity** is a stronger condition, meaning that the institution's assets deliver a **cash flow** allowing it to pay its liabilities *on time*. If a firm is liquid, it is solvent, but it might be solvent while illiquid.

Some writers suggest that "prudent" banks will invest in short-term assets, in order to remain liquid. Yet by their very nature, banks issuing fiduciary media are illiquid: their liabilities are immediately due if presented, while their assets are necessarily of longer duration. The best such banks can strive for is solvency.

## 6. The Significance of Short-Term Cover

Sometimes legislation, but always public opinion, compels the banks to give preference to short-term rather than long-term loans. This is a quite valid preference, backed up by centuries of experience. However, the explanation for its wisdom is *not* that it allows the banks to redeem fiduciary media in the event of a panic—the bank's asset maturities are irrelevant if everyone shows up, demanding redemption. The actual benefit from focusing bank loans on short-term investments is simply that the constraint checks the bank's ability to issue fiduciary media.

## 7. The Security of the Investments of the Credit-Issuing Banks

There is similar confusion when it comes to proposals seeking to guarantee the (eventual) redemption of all fiduciary media by means of reserve funds consisting of illiquid assets (such as mortgages). Even if the public is certain that they will be *eventually* paid in money (in the narrower sense) for the claims to money that they currently hold, even so, if there is any doubt about the *immediacy* of the payment, then the claims will no longer be money substitutes. Instead, the public will take into account the delay before receiving payment, and such claims will trade at a discount to the money itself. (Note that if the claims continue to circulate as generally accepted media of exchange, even though everyone knows that redemption at best will occur after some delay, then the claims will have become credit money.)

## 8. Foreign Bills of Exchange as a Component of the Redemption Fund

A bank cannot increase its issue of money substitutes (consisting of both money certificates and fiduciary media) beyond the demand of its own clientele, for use in their dealings with each other. However, to the extent that sometimes its clients need to exchange their money substitutes when dealing with *foreign* citizens, the bank has the option of keeping some of its reserve fund in the form of *foreign* money substitutes, as opposed to money in the narrower sense. (This is because the foreigners with whom the bank's clients wish to do business, will accept money substitutes issued by institutions from their respective countries.) Yet this practice means that the original bank's reserve fund has a smaller proportion of money in the narrower sense, and hence that its own money substitutes consist of a higher fraction of fiduciary media (versus money certificates).

## *Technical Notes*

- In modern times, one of the major controversies within the Austrian School concerns the legitimacy of fractional reserve banking. Some Austrians follow Murray Rothbard who argued that bank issuance of fiduciary media leads to the boom-bust cycle and is inherently fraudulent—akin to a warehouse manager renting out the goods that were supposedly placed with him for safekeeping. Other Austrians such as George Selgin and Steve Horwitz call their position "**free banking**" and believe that there is no reason for banks to necessarily keep 100 percent reserves of money in the narrower sense, in order to fully cover all outstanding customer deposits. The free bankers argue that market forces will determine the proper ratio of money certificates to fiduciary media in a competitive banking system. (Virtually all modern Austrians agree that government-sponsored *central banking* and *fiat currency* are both economically destructive and morally illegitimate. The dispute concerns the proper practice of private banks operating in a laissez-faire environment.)

- Continuing with the above note, both groups point to passages in Mises's writings to lend credence to their position. Even within this very chapter, Mises offers statements that—viewed in isolation—would seem to definitively side with one camp versus the other. (Two of these quotations are the opening selections for the study questions below.) Although Mises agrees with the Rothbardian, 100-percent-reserve camp that there is a paradox in the very nature of what fiduciary media claim to be, on the other hand he also agrees with the free bankers that the historical development of fiduciary media economized on resources (that would have otherwise gone into the socially wasteful production of more gold and silver for monetary purposes). Thus Mises does not clearly fall into one camp or the other. (Of course Mises's own view wouldn't settle the modern dispute: he could have been simply mistaken, regardless of his position.)

## *New Terminology*

**Free banking (among modern Austrians):** The doctrine holding that a free market in banking will pick the optimal fraction of reserves, which may be below 100 percent. Free banking theorists do not believe that the issue of fiduciary media per se causes the business cycle, only that excess quantities of fiduciary media do, and that such an outcome is almost always associated with government-supported issues of fiduciary media.

**Solvency:** The situation in which the market value of an institution's assets exceeds its liabilities.

**Liquidity:** The situation in which an institution's assets will deliver a cash flow allowing it to pay its liabilities on time. (All liquid enterprises are also solvent, but not necessarily vice versa.)

**Cash flow:** The stream of money payments over time due to an asset or collection of assets.

**Hypothecary loans:** Loans granted with an asset such as real estate serving as collateral.

## *Study Questions*

1. Explain: "Thus there lies an irresolvable contradiction in the nature of fiduciary media. Their equivalence to money depends on the promise that they will at any time be converted into money at the demand of the person entitled to them and on the fact that proper precautions are taken to make this promise effective. But—and this is likewise involved in the nature of fiduciary media—what is promised is an impossibility in so far as the bank is never able to keep its loans perfectly liquid." (p. 322)

2. Explain: "The issue of fiduciary media has made it possible to avoid the convulsions that would be involved in an increase in the objective exchange value of money, and reduced the cost of the monetary apparatus." (p. 323)

3. When Mises says of coins that their "smooth faces tell no tales of the methods by which they have been acquired," is he making an argument for or against the possibility of customers paying banks for providing them with (fully-backed) deposit and checkbook services? (p. 324)

4. Why does Mises say that a single bank with no competitors, or an industry of banks operating with uniform policies, would suffer no limitations on their ability to issue fiduciary media? (pp. 325–26)

5. Explain: "Whether the assets of a credit-issuing bank consist of short-term bills or of **hypothecary loans** remains a matter of indifference in the case of a general run." (p. 333)

CHAPTER 19

# MONEY, CREDIT, AND INTEREST

## *Chapter Outline*

### 1. On the Nature of the Problem

**Interest** accrues as the difference between what a producer pays upfront for inputs versus the total revenue he receives for the product (down the road). Up till now in the book, we have studied the forces that can change the exchange ratio between money and consumer goods, or what are called **goods of the first order**. Now we will investigate whether changes in the supply of and demand for money can affect the money-prices of **goods of higher orders** (i.e., producer goods) to a different extent.

Tooke, Fullarton, and other members of the Banking School thought that the banks had no power to influence prices, because any excess issue of fiduciary media would be immediately returned to them. Yet Lord Overstone, Torrens, and other members of the Currency School thought otherwise. They correctly recognized that by lowering the rate of interest, the banks could induce the public to accept more fiduciary media. This is the mechanism through which bank credit policy can influence the purchasing power of money and the rate of interest.

## 2. The Connexion Between Variations in the Ratio Between the Stock of Money and the Demand for Money and Fluctuations in the Rate of Interest

There are three senses in which variations in the stock of and demand for money can influence the rate of interest. First, in the case of metallic currency, such variations can *directly* affect the rate of interest by directly affecting the **subsistence fund**. For example, a fall in the demand to hold gold as money, will release gold into industrial purposes and thereby make the community wealthier, in the same sense as if the amount of wheat stored in silos had increased.

Variations in the stock of and demand for money can influence the rate of interest *indirectly* and in the long run, by permanently changing the distribution of property and income. For example, a reduction in the stock of money could redistribute wealth into the hands of creditors, who tend to save more. Thus the rate of interest would be permanently lower because the overall rate of saving would have increased.

Finally, variations can influence the rate of interest in the short run as prices adjust to the new realities of the stock of and demand for money. When prices are generally rising, the rate of interest tends to be higher, as entrepreneurs are willing and able to offer more to borrow money. (Nowadays this is called a **purchasing power** or **inflation premium** in the contractual rate of interest.) When prices are falling, the rate of interest tends to be lower.

## 3. The Connexion Between the Equilibrium Rate and the Money Rate of Interest

When the banks issue more fiduciary media, the immediate result is a reduction in the rate of interest. Because the banks typically invest the new issue themselves, or lend it to businesses for productive investment, the subsistence fund tends to increase and the rate of interest will remain *permanently* lower than the original level (though not as low as it was after its initial drop). However, there is no quantitative relationship between the amount of new fiduciary media issued, and the fall in the interest rate. Indeed, no matter how much new money the banks create and lend out, they will never force the contractual rate of interest below zero percent.

The gratuitous nature of credit refers to the fact that the banks can push down the rate of interest apparently at will. Are there any forces tending to reestablish the natural premium of present versus future goods? Wicksell argued that if the banks push the Money Rate of Interest below the Natural Rate of Interest, that forces will eventually restore the Money Rate back to the Natural Rate. But his argument for why this should occur is unsatisfactory.

## 4. The Influence of the Interest Policy of the Credit-Issuing Banks on Production

As Böhm-Bawerk explained [see Technical Notes], the rate of interest governs the time for which resources are "tied up" in production processes. The lower the rate of interest, the longer the processes that entrepreneurs will select. In equilibrium, the money rate of interest equals the natural rate, and entrepreneurs invest resources in processes such that their fruits (consumption goods) are completed just as the available savings (subsistence fund) is exhausted. It is technically possible to lengthen the structure of production, but without additional savings, the subsistence fund will not be able to feed the workers while they labor in the longer processes.

When the banks lower the money rate of interest by issuing fiduciary media, they induce entrepreneurs to act as if the subsistence fund had really grown (when in fact it has not). Entrepreneurs borrow money at the lower rates, hire workers, and try to bid away resources from others to begin longer-term processes. A general boom period ensues, where most people feel prosperous.

Yet because the issue of fiduciary media doesn't actually make society richer, the boom must necessarily come to an end. There are physically not enough savings to carry society forward, until the time when the new (longer) processes yield their final consumption goods. A bust (what we now call a recession) sets in. As the output of consumption goods declines, their prices rise. Realizing their errors, the entrepreneurs discontinue those projects that were only apparently profitable, because of the false interest rate. The prices of producer goods fall, and the money rate of interest returns to the natural rate.

## 5. Credit and Economic Crises

In practice, the bust occurs when the banks slow down their issue of further fiduciary media, thereby allowing the money rate to rise toward its proper level. Yet even if the banks stubbornly tried to hold the money rate down, eventually they would fail. The growing expansion of the quantity of money in the broader sense drives prices higher and higher, and lenders insist on greater and greater premiums in the contractual rate of interest. The longer the banks hold the money rate below the natural rate, the worse is the eventual crisis.

## *Technical Notes*

- Eugen von Böhm-Bawerk was a successor of Menger and a predecessor of Mises in the development of Austrian economics. One of Böhm-Bawerk's great contributions was to explain the capitalists' interest income as a premium given to present versus future goods. For example, suppose consumers would pay $50 for a mature Christmas tree, but would only pay $40 for an airtight claim guaranteeing them a mature Christmas tree to be delivered in twelve months. If these were the final prices as determined by consumers' subjective preferences, then the market price for an *immature* tree—one that needed another year to fully develop—would be $40 as well. Assuming nothing else changed, a capitalist who invested $40 in such a tree could wait one year, then sell the mature version for $50, netting a 25 percent annual return on his capital. Thus Böhm-Bawerk explained the ability to earn interest over time as due to the underlying subjective preference for present versus future goods. A capitalist who buys factors of production invests in "future goods" which then grow in market value as they ripen into "present goods." Also note that the term "ripen" is not reserved for agricultural products: Böhm-Bawerk would say that a capitalist can invest (say) $100,000 in lumber, shingles, labor, and other inputs which represent a future house. Over the months, as the house is built, the goods-in-process gradually become a present house, and hence command a higher market value than the initial $100,000 investment.

- In explaining the boom and bust cycle, Mises relies on Böhm-Bawerk's capital theory. Böhm-Bawerk viewed the use of capital goods as a "roundabout" way of satisfying goals. For example, if someone wants to get coconuts from tree branches, a direct approach is to climb the tree and grab them with his bare hands. Yet a more roundabout (and physically productive) approach is to spend some time gathering sticks and vines, in order to construct a long pole. Then with this capital good, the person can knock down far more coconuts per hour of his labor. The tradeoff then is between getting more physical output per unit of labor, versus getting the coconuts sooner rather than later. (If the person is ravenous and wants to eat a few coconuts as quickly as possible, he will just climb the tree rather than search for sticks.) Böhm-Bawerk argued that the rate of interest reflected the community's preferences for the timing of consumption as well as the technical opportunities for increased output resulting from further lengthening (or making more roundabout) the methods of production. If some people in the community saved more (by stockpiling coconuts, say), then the workers would be able to eat while production shifted out of tree-climbing and into pole-production. The savings would have augmented the subsistence fund to tide everyone over until the higher output of the more roundabout processes came online. The rate of interest in this scenario would permanently decline, and society would advance to a permanently higher standard of living, as workers could gather more coconuts per hour with the use of their new tools.

## *New Terminology*

**Interest:** Income accruing to the owner of future goods as they mature into present goods, due to the higher valuation placed on present versus future goods.

**Goods of the first order:** Consumer goods.

**Goods of higher orders:** Goods used to produce consumer goods. (A capital good used to produce a consumer good is a second-order good. A capital good used to produce a second-order good is a third-order good, etc.)

**Subsistence fund:** A concept used by Böhm-Bawerk to denote the savings the capitalists must have first accumulated, in order to feed and otherwise support the workers as they engage in time-consuming production processes.

**Purchasing power/inflation premium:** An increase in the contractual rate of interest due to the expected rise in prices.

## *Study Questions*

1. What is "the problem," the nature of which is outlined in section 1? (pp. 339–46)

2. Why might the distribution of income and property alter the long-run rate of interest? (p. 347)

3. If the Money Rate of Interest is pushed below the Natural Rate of Interest (or more accurately, the normal rate of interest), what happens to commodity prices, according to Wicksell? (p. 355)

4. What are the two main mechanisms by which the money rate of interest rises back to the natural rate, after having been pushed down by the banks? (pp. 362–63)

5. Explain: "Certainly, the banks would be able to *postpone* the collapse; but nevertheless . . . the moment must eventually come when no further extension of the circulation of fiduciary media is possible. Then the catastrophe occurs. . . ." (p. 365)

CHAPTER 20

# PROBLEMS OF CREDIT POLICY

## *Summary*

The governments of Europe and America have been guided by the idea that the natural desire of the banks to issue fiduciary media must be checked, in order to avoid economic crises. However, this goal conflicts with the other desires for low interest rates and high selling prices.

Peel's Bank Act [Bank Charter Act 1844] took the power of issuing new notes away from private banks and vested it completely with the Bank of England, which itself was required to maintain 100 percent metallic backing for any new notes that it issued. However, the Act crucially did *not* impose such a restriction on the extension of deposits. Peel's Act thus contained a "safety valve" that prevented a sharp rise in the objective exchange value of money, but at the same time it failed to eliminate economic crises because it erroneously thought they were due exclusively to unbacked *notes*.

The degradation of the classical gold standard was already well underway *before* the outbreak of World War I. First, citizens ceased using gold in everyday transactions, and the actual gold was stockpiled in the vaults of each country's central bank, which issued paper notes instead. Then the gold was even further concentrated into the central banks of just a few major countries, so that not even the central banks (of most countries) had gold in their vaults. Although it would have undesirable deflationary consequences, a transition back to an actual gold currency—in which people used genuine gold coins in daily purchases—is the only realistic check on government-sponsored inflation.

The original étatist arguments for regulating the issue of competing notes by private banks do not look nearly as compelling after the experience of German hyperinflation. The alleged evils of a free market in banking are nothing compared to the actual evils under a government monopoly of the currency.

People must choose between a fiat system regulated by index numbers of prices, or a return to an actual gold currency. In order to prevent recurring economic crises, the absolute prohibition of the further issuance of fiduciary media is necessary. If banks continue with the ability to issue fiduciary media, it leaves open the destruction of the entire monetary system, as a coordinated policy of expansion—perhaps under a World Bank—would have no checks on its inflationary potential.

## *Chapter Outline*

# I. PREFATORY REMARK

### 1. The Conflict of Credit Policies

Since the time of the Currency School, the governments of Europe and America have been guided by the idea that the natural desire of the banks to issue fiduciary media must be checked, in order to avoid economic crises. However, this goal conflicts with the other desires to foster "cheap money" and "reasonable prices," i.e., low interest rates and high prices for certain producers.

# II. PROBLEMS OF CREDIT POLICY BEFORE THE WAR

### 2. Peel's Act

Peel's Bank Act [Bank Charter Act 1844] took the power of issuing new notes away from private banks and vested it completely with the Bank of England, which itself was required to maintain 100 percent metallic backing for any new notes that it issued. However, the Act crucially did *not* impose such a restriction on the extension of deposits. In other words, private banks could create more fiduciary media by granting loans (not backed by gold) to their customers, thus lowering the rate of interest and expanding the stock of money in the broader sense. In this way, Peel's Act contained a "safety valve" that prevented a sharp rise in the objective exchange value of money (i.e., falling prices of goods and services), but at the same time it failed to eliminate economic crises because it erroneously thought they were due exclusively to unbacked *notes*.

## 3. The Nature of Discount Policy

Many writers, as well as the general public, do not understand the "real" economic forces behind movements in interest rates; instead they view increases in interest rates as arbitrary and unnecessary constraints on the community's prosperity. For example, it is in the nature of banking that an individual bank must raise the interest rate it charges on new loans, if its reserves of money in the narrower sense are being drained because it has issued more fiduciary media than its competitors. This behavior would occur whether or not government or central bank rules required it.

When it comes to international movements of capital, people also fail to understand that domestic interest rates must reflect conditions in the world market. There is nothing more mysterious in foreign events altering domestic interest rates, than (say) a foreign crop failure raising domestic fruit prices.

## 4. The Gold-Premium Policy

The Bank of France implemented a well-known gold-premium policy, in which it charged a premium (somewhere in the range of 0.4 to 0.8 percent) on requests to exchange francs for gold, if the gold were going to be invested abroad seeking a higher return. The purpose of the policy was to widen the gap by which the Bank of France could maintain a lower discount rate than prevailed in other countries. The policy hindered capital outflows *and* inflows, and hindered the full incorporation of France into the world market. The only way to truly insulate Bank policy from the rest of the world market would be to leave the gold standard entirely, adopting credit money or fiat money and thereby suffering inflation.

## 5. Systems Similar to the Gold-Premium Policy

Central banks have adopted other techniques to hinder the export of gold. For example, they might not surrender gold to exporters in the most convenient form, or they might give worn-out coins that had slightly less metal content than the coins intended for domestic use.

## 6. The Non-Satisfaction of the So-called "Illegitimate" Demand for Money

Attempts to only provide gold for export when the purpose is "legitimate" would fail to achieve their objective in the long-term, as speculators would find other means to achieve the same end. Moreover, there is a whole spectrum of intermediate cases between "legitimate" demands for commodity importation and "illegitimate" speculation on foreign investments. For example, what if a foreign company wanted to withdraw deposits that it had previously invested in a country? Would the authorities permit a "loss" of gold in this circumstance?

## 7. Other Measures for Strengthening the Stock of Metal Held by the Central Banks-of-Issue

While central banks-of-issue adopted policies to raise the **upper gold point** and thus discourage the export of gold, at the same time many adopted policies to reduce the **lower gold point** and thus encourage imports of gold. The two sets of policies largely offset each other, so that the actual gap between the gold points did not change as much as might have been supposed.

### 8. The Promotion of Cheque and Clearing Transactions as a Means of Reducing the Rate of Discount

In Germany before the first World War, there was an effort to reduce the German people's everyday use of gold, and replace it with the use of check and clearing transactions. This would allegedly allow the Reichsbank to hold a larger reserve of metal, and keep a lower discount rate. However, there is no necessary connection between the long-run rate of interest and the quantity of fiduciary media.

## III. PROBLEMS OF CREDIT POLICY IN THE PERIOD IMMEDIATELY AFTER THE WAR

### 9. The Gold-Exchange Standard

During the World War I, the major powers (except the United States) explicitly suspended the gold standard. However, the degradation of the classical gold standard was already well underway *before* the outbreak of war. First, citizens ceased using gold in everyday transactions, and the actual gold was stockpiled in the vaults of each country's central bank, which issued paper notes instead. Then the gold was even further concentrated into the central banks of just a few major countries, so that not even the central banks (of most countries) had gold in their vaults. Instead, they too had paper claims entitling them to the gold that was stored elsewhere.

In this way, virtually the entire world became accustomed to using paper as their money, which had a more and more tenuous link to gold. As of 1924, the world price of gold was dominated by the actions of the United States government. Yet such an outcome is the antithesis of the whole rationale for the gold standard: to keep political interference out of money.

## 10. A Return to a Gold Currency

Although it would have undesirable deflationary consequences, a transition back to an actual gold currency—in which people used genuine gold coins in daily purchases—is the only realistic check on government-sponsored inflation. Had the citizens of the great powers been using gold on the eve of World War I, it would have been much more difficult for their governments to run the printing presses to pay for armaments.

## 11. The Problem of the Freedom of the Banks

The original étatist arguments for regulating the issue of competing notes by private banks do not look nearly as compelling after the experience of German hyperinflation. The alleged evils of a free market in banking are nothing compared to the actual evils under a government monopoly of the currency.

## 12. Fisher's Proposal for a Commodity Standard

The famous American economist Irving Fisher proposed that index numbers would track an average of commodity prices, so that the dollar itself could be defined as a variable weight of gold that possessed constant purchasing power in terms of the commodities in the index.

There are several problems with Fisher's proposal. First, the various index numbers are arbitrary; there is no scientific way to measure the "true" change in the purchasing power of gold from month to month. Another problem is that the market already has techniques for handling changes in the purchasing power of money; Fisher's proposal would simply lead to an adjustment of the techniques. Finally, even ignoring the other problems, Fisher's proposal would not counteract the *differential* impact that inflation has as it unevenly spreads through the economy. If the price index increases by 1 percent in a certain month, this is because some prices increased by more than 1 percent, while others increased by less.

## 13. The Basic Questions of Future Currency Policy

People must choose between a fiat system regulated by index numbers of prices, or a return to an actual gold currency. In order to prevent recurring economic crises, the absolute prohibition of the further issuance of fiduciary media is necessary. (Such a prohibition must go beyond Peel's Act, and include bank deposits as well as notes, for economically the two are equivalent.) If banks continue with the ability to issue fiduciary media, it leaves open the destruction of the entire monetary system, as a coordinated policy of expansion—perhaps under a World Bank—would have no checks on its inflationary potential.

Only by freeing money and banking from political influence can people avoid economic crises while maintaining the highest possible stability of the purchasing power of money.

## *Technical Notes*

- On pages 377–82, Mises describes the "gold-premium policy" implemented by the Bank of France. In the absence of such a premium, investors wouldn't distinguish between domestic and foreign investments (except perhaps for a slight psychological preference for the former), and would put their capital where it would earn the highest return. If the Bank of England's discount rate were higher than the Bank of France's, then French investors would turn their francs in for gold, use the gold to buy bonds in England, then convert the gold back into francs after earning their interest. The result would be a higher rate of return (measured in francs) than if the investors had lent the money in France. However, if turning francs into gold involves payment of a (small) premium to the Bank of France, then investors would only adopt the above strategy if the difference in interest rates were sufficiently large. Therefore, the gold-premium policy gave the Bank of France a wider margin to keep interest rates relatively low, before suffering from an outflow of gold.

- On page 398, Mises points out that most arguments criticizing the operation of a private, competitive banking system were "thoroughly unsound." The one legitimate argument came from the Currency School, which (correctly) pointed out that if private banks issued notes in excess of their gold reserves (i.e., fiduciary media), this could cause economic crises. Ironically, this danger only exists when the banks all operate under a uniform discount policy—they must all inflate in unison, or else the bank that is the most aggressive will have its fiduciary media returned to it (through clearing operations), and it will quickly lose its gold reserve to its competitors. Yet somehow, these observations led to the call to abolish competitive banknote issue and replace it with a government monopoly. As Mises says, "Now the monopolization of the banks-of-issue in each separate country does not merely fail to oppose any hindrance of this uniformity of procedure; it materially facilitates it."

## *New Terminology*

**Upper gold point:** Under the gold standard, the maximum market price of gold (quoted in a country's currency) above which it is profitable—including all costs of transport, re-coinage, etc.—for foreigners to exchange the domestic currency for gold (at the official redemption rate, which is below the current market price), and have the gold shipped out of the original country.

**Lower gold point:** Under the gold standard, the minimum market price of gold (quoted in a country's currency) beneath which it is profitable—including all costs of transport, re-coinage, etc.—for citizens to import gold and exchange it with the authorities at the official redemption rate for the domestic currency.

## *Study Questions*

1. What was the theoretical error of the Currency School, and why was this mistake an "advantage" with respect to the implementation of Peel's Act? (pp. 369–70)

*2. When Mises claims that a sole bank, engaging in a more inflationary policy than its competitors, would endanger its "solvency" (p. 374), is that consistent with his definition of the term (versus "liquidity") on page 331?

3. Explain: "The banks would still have to have a discount policy even if there were no legislative regulation of the note cover." (p. 374)

4. How did France's gold-premium policy hinder both the outflow *and* inflow of capital? (p. 382)

5. Explain: "There is only one danger that is peculiar to the issue of notes; that of its being released from the common-law obligation under which everybody who enters into a commitment is strictly required to fulfill it at all times and in all places. This danger is infinitely greater and more threatening under a system of monopoly." (p. 399)

PART IV

# MONETARY RECONSTRUCTION

CHAPTER 21

# THE PRINCIPLE OF SOUND MONEY

*Chapter Outline*

## 1. The Classical Idea of Sound Money

The principle of sound money must be placed in the context of the broader, classical liberal program of containing government tyranny. Just as a constitution or a bill of rights would be adopted, in light of historical abuses of civil liberties, in the same way the classical liberals of the nineteenth century wanted to prevent governments from wrecking currencies as had occurred throughout history.

Sound money involves a metallic standard, with all tokens and paper notes being redeemable in the metallic money upon demand. In practice, this has meant gold since the late nineteenth century.

Although their ideas were correct, the classical liberals did not adequately defend the gold standard from its critics, and the public fell sway to erroneous inflationary doctrines.

## 2. The Virtues and Alleged Shortcomings of the Gold Standard

It is true that the public generally welcomes inflationism as opposed to the orthodoxy of the gold standard, but only because they misunderstand the true situation. Producers welcome "high prices" when it is their own prices in question, but they don't welcome increasing prices in the items they themselves must purchase. Inflation can only give even the appearance of prosperity, in situations where the majority don't recognize what is happening. For this reason, inflationism cannot be a lasting economic policy.

Contrary to its critics, the gold standard did not "collapse." Rather, it was systematically and intentionally destroyed by governments bent on inflation. Those writers who blame the "rules of the gold standard game" for keeping interest rates high, do not understand the function of interest rates and how credit expansion causes economic booms and busts.

## 3. The Full-Employment Doctrine

An employer will only hire a man if he is productive enough to justify the wage he expects to be paid. If the employer would lose money by hiring the man, he will remain unemployed. When government policies and unions use coercion to hold wage rates above the market-clearing level, **institutional unemployment** results.

In this setting, it is true that monetary inflation may cause commodity prices to rise faster than wage rates. This will decrease the unemployment rate, but only because it effectively lowers the workers' **real wages**. Once the labor unions realize what is happening, they will begin demanding automatic wage increases tied to the "cost of living." Then the apparent benefits of inflation (in reducing unemployment) will disappear.

## 4. The Emergency Argument in Favor of Inflation

Some writers concede the negative effects of inflation, but argue that in certain emergency situations, it is the only method by which governments can carry out vital tasks. Yet inflation per se does not increase the physical and human resources at a country's disposal. If an apologist for inflation claims that it is the only way to finance a war, he is admitting that the public would not agree with the government's war expenditures if it fully understood the sacrifice they would entail.

## *Important Contributions*

- On pages 420–21 Mises responds to a critique of the gold standard that its opponents continue to use. Modern-day critics still say (as they did in Mises's time) that the gold standard "collapsed" and that governments are no longer willing to play the "rules of the gold standard game." What they mean is that governments were no longer willing to renounce the (short-term) benefits to themselves of inflation, and so they refused to redeem their currencies in specie. Yet Mises points out that the governments did much more than this. In order to wean the public off gold, they employed "policemen, customs guards, penal courts, prisons, in some countries even executioners." In Mises's view, governments actively combat the public's preference for a sound commodity money. Contrary to the claims of the inflationists, maintenance of a commodity money doesn't require a special commitment from the government, but rather requires only that the government obey its contractual obligations like everybody else in a market economy.

- On pages 423–26, Mises places Keynesian analysis in a tradition of faulty theories going back to the "spurious grocer philosophy ... exploded by Adam Smith and Jean-Baptist Say." These classical economists argued that a general business depression was *not* caused by a "dearness of money," and consequently could not be solved by monetary inflation. Say's discussion (which later came to be summarized as "Say's Law") explained that ultimately, the grocer's customers earned the purchasing power to demand his products by first supplying their own goods and services. As an economy grew over time, the various sectors increased their output across the board. Say argued that relative prices would adjust to maintain the proper balance among the sectors, but there was not a danger that the economy as a whole could produce a "general glut" that could only be remedied by an expansion of the stock of money.

## *New Terminology*

**Institutional unemployment:** The situation where workers are qualified and willing to accept jobs at prevailing wage rates, yet cannot find employers to hire them.

**Real wages:** Wage rates relative to the prices of goods and services.

## *Study Questions*

1. What was the "serious blunder" of the nineteenth-century advocates of the gold standard? (p. 415)

2. What connection does Mises make between the gold standard and representative government? (p. 416)

3. How did governments manage to abandon the gold standard? (p. 420)

4. What is the only efficacious way to raise real wage rates? (p. 424)

5. What's wrong with the emergency argument in favor of inflation? (pp. 426–28)

CHAPTER 22

# CONTEMPORARY CURRENCY SYSTEMS

*Chapter Outline*

## 1. The Inflexible Gold Standard

Under both the **classical gold standard** and the **gold-exchange standard**—as they had existed before World War I—each nation's currency unit was legally tied to an inflexible (i.e., constant) exchange rate against gold. The difference between the two systems was one of degree. Under the classical gold standard, citizens within each country carried actual gold coins and used them in everyday transactions. Anybody could exchange gold for national notes and vice versa without delay. Later, under the gold-exchange standard, citizens only used the government's paper notes and token coins in domestic commerce. However, the central banks of the world still exchanged their respective currencies against gold at the official (and inflexible) rates.

## 2. The Flexible Standard

The **flexible standard** arose between the world wars out of the prewar gold exchange standard. Here there was no legal redemption requirement, locking in a fixed exchange rate of gold against the national currency. Instead, an agency (such as the central bank) would be given the authority to **peg** the currency to gold at a rate that could be subject to a sudden change. If the drop in the currency against gold was severe enough, the event would be called a **devaluation**.

## 3. The Freely-Vacillating Currency

A **freely-vacillating currency** is one with no official peg to gold at all. The currency is a credit or fiat money, held on account of its expected future purchasing power. If the government exercises restraint, such a money—even though it is a "bad currency"—can persist.

## 4. The Illusive Standard

Sometimes a government will announce a (variable) peg to its currency, yet this isn't a flexible standard. The government enforces the peg through penalties and confiscation, not through redemption at the official rate. The **illusive standard** is thus a form of price control, and leads to a shortage in the foreign exchange market.

## *Technical Notes*

- As Mises explained earlier in the book (pp. 180–86), exchange rates adjust on an unhampered market until there is no advantage to buying a commodity in one currency and immediately selling it in another currency. Yet under an illusive standard, the government of a country actively interferes with this process, often to keep the price of its own currency above the market-clearing price that would achieve purchasing power parity. In Mises's example (p. 434), the market clears when one dollar trades for 100 Ruritanian rurs. If a barrel of oil (say) sells for $100 in the United States, and for 10,000 rurs in Ruritania, there is no arbitrage opportunity at the correct exchange rate. However, if the Ruritanian government announces that it will put people in prison who pay more than 50 rurs for one dollar, then the exchange rate will rise to the artificial price (at least within the borders of Ruritania). At the new exchange rate, oil purchased abroad will now only cost 5,000 rurs per barrel, compared to the domestic price of 10,000 rurs. Ruritanian refiners will thus try to sell their rurs against dollars, in order to buy oil and import it. However, foreigners will not want to sell many dollars for rurs at the ratio of 1-to-50, because the actual market ratio is 1-to-100. Consequently the Ruritanian refiners will complain that they "can't find dollars" to finance their desired imports. There is an apparent "shortage of dollars."

- After explaining the mechanics of **foreign-exchange controls**, Mises on page 434 classifies them as "a device for the virtual expropriation of foreign investments." He has in mind a scenario such as the following: Suppose a U.S. capitalist invests $1 million building a factory in Ruritania. At the original, market-determined exchange rate, the capitalist sells his $1 million for 100 million rurs, and uses the currency to buy materials, hire workers, etc. in Ruritania to set up the factory. Every year the factory earns a net income of 5 million rurs. The foreign owner would have his local agents sell the 5 million rurs in the foreign exchange market, converting them to $50,000, and wiring the money back to his bank account in the United States. Thus from either the viewpoint of the factory manager (reckoning in rurs) or from the foreign investor (reckoning in dollars), the rate of return on the invested capital is five percent per year. However, when the Ruritanian government imposes foreign-exchange controls and sets a new price of $1 for 50 rurs (instead of 100), the market for dollars dries up. Now when the factory earns its usual 5 million rurs, the American investor can't get the money out of the country. It's true that officially speaking, his 5 million rurs is now worth $100,000, double the previous amount. But this is little consolation, since no one with dollars will actually trade $100,000 for 5 million rurs. People around the world would be willing to trade half that ($50,000) for 5 million rurs, but the Ruritanian government will punish any of its citizens caught accepting such an offer. Thus the American's $1 million factory in Ruritania has effectively been taken over by the Ruritanian government, since it controls the foreign-exchange market, and converting rurs into dollars is the only way the American owner can derive any benefit from his investment.

## *New Terminology*

**Classical gold standard:** The system by which a country's currency is redeemable on demand for a fixed weight of gold. In Mises's usage, under a classical gold standard, a portion of the citizens' cash balances consists of actual gold coins and bullion to be used for making purchases.

**Gold-exchange standard:** The system by which a country's currency is redeemable on demand for a fixed weight of gold, though sometimes only by other governments and central banks. In Mises's usage, under a gold-exchange standard the citizens used only paper notes in everyday transactions, while the actual gold was stored in bank or government vaults.

**Flexible standard:** The system by which a country's currency is redeemable for a variable weight of gold, to be announced by the government at its discretion.

**Currency peg:** The variable and nonlegally-binding rate at which a government is currently maintaining its currency's exchange rate against gold.

**Devaluation:** The situation in which a country on the flexible standard announces a large drop in the value of its currency against gold.

**Freely-vacillating currency:** A credit or fiat currency that has no official peg to gold at all. Its market price fluctuates just as any commodity.

**Illusive standard:** The system by which a country's currency is pegged to gold at nonmarket rates. The exchange rate is maintained not through the manipulation of gold reserves but rather through the enforcement of foreign-exchange controls.

**Foreign-exchange controls:** Government restrictions on the market for foreign currencies.

## *Study Questions*

1. Under the classical and gold exchange standards, did it matter if banknotes were endowed with legal tender status? (p. 429)

2. Why did the unorthodox statesman prefer the term "peg" to "redemption"? (p. 430)

*3. Mises says (p. 431) that credit and fiat moneys "are not money substitutes but money proper in themselves." Does this mean that commodity money is not money proper?

4. What is the outstanding instance of a freely-vacillating currency? (p. 431)

5. Why does Mises dislike the term "scarcity of foreign exchange"? (pp. 433–34)

CHAPTER 23

# THE RETURN TO SOUND MONEY

## *Summary*

The disintegration of the worldwide classical gold standard has gone hand-in-hand with the march toward all-round central planning. The return to sound money involves a renunciation of inflation. This is only possible if the public recognizes the futility of interventionist government.

The return to sound money still means a return to the gold standard. Only under this system will the determination of the monetary unit's purchasing power remain outside the sphere of government control. The only way to truly safeguard a nation's money is to remove all avenues for inflation. This includes not only the government's resorting to the printing press to finance its deficits, but also commercial banks' ability to issue deposits not fully backed up by money proper.

For a relatively small country ("Ruritania") the government of which has been using inflation to finance its deficits, the government must first (temporarily) prohibit the further issuance of fiduciary media denominated in "rurs." Once the rur's exchange rate (as well as the price of gold quoted in rurs) has clearly peaked, the government of Ruritania locks in the current market price of either a U.S. dollar or gold (quoted in rurs). An agency will be dedicated with the sole task of maintaining the rur's redemption rate to either the dollar or gold at this rate, forever. Ruritania will be back on the gold exchange standard.

The United States government must return to the classical gold standard. An agency will be established that will buy or sell gold against dollars upon demand, at this rate. In order to provide more resistance to future inflation, the government should suppress small-denomination paper notes, which would force Americans to once again carry full-weight gold coins in their cash balances.

Only an abandonment of the interventionist mindset, coupled with a return to the classical gold standard, can safeguard the currency.

## Chapter Outline

### 1. Monetary Policy and the Present Trend Toward All-Round Planning

The disintegration of the worldwide classical gold standard has gone hand-in-hand with the march toward all-round central planning. The trends are related. Inflation allows government officials to seize control of more resources than the public would otherwise approve. Rising prices pushes people into higher tax brackets and allows the government to tax "excess profits" from businesses. The social unrest caused by inflation can be blamed upon capitalism, giving the government yet another pretext to expand its power.

The return to sound money involves a renunciation of inflation. This is only possible if the public recognizes the futility of interventionist government.

### 2. The Integral Gold Standard

The return to sound money still means a return to the gold standard. Only under this system will the determination of the monetary unit's purchasing power remain outside the sphere of government control.

The only way to truly safeguard a nation's money is to remove all avenues for inflation. This includes not only the government's resorting to the printing press to finance its deficits, but also commercial banks' ability to issue deposits not fully backed up by money proper. In other words, governments must spend only what they tax or borrow, and banks must be prohibited from issuing new fiduciary media.

## 3. Currency Reform in Ruritania

For a relatively small country the government of which has been using inflation to finance its deficits, the crucial thing is to quickly assure world investors that the currency is stabilized. There is a two-step process involved. First, the government of Ruritania must (temporarily) prohibit the further issuance of fiduciary media denominated in "rurs," the currency of the country. This will cause the exchange rate of the rur to stop falling against other, major currencies as well as gold.

Once the rur's exchange rate (as well as the price of gold quoted in rurs) has clearly peaked, and begun a definite downward trend, it is time for step two. In this stage, the government of Ruritania locks in the current market price of either a U.S. dollar or gold (quoted in rurs). An agency will be dedicated with the sole task of maintaining the rur's redemption rate to either the dollar or gold at this rate, forever. If people turn in dollars or gold (depending on the choice of the link), the agency is allowed to issue new rurs, which are backed up 100 percent by the new deposit. At this point, the rur will be back on either a dollar- or gold-exchange standard, and no new fiduciary media can be issued.

## 4. The United States' Return to a Sound Currency

The United States government must return to the classical gold standard, which offered a stronger check on inflation than the gold-exchange standard. It must first prohibit the issuance of new dollars, whether in the form of Treasury notes or bank balances not backed up 100 percent by cash deposits. After the dollar-price of gold stabilizes, the U.S. government will announce the current market price as the new, permanent exchange rate between the U.S. dollar and gold. (The new price might very well be higher than the official rate of $35 per ounce, established in the Bretton

Woods agreement near the end of World War II, and lasting until Richard Nixon abolished the last remnants of the gold standard in 1971.)

An agency will be established that will buy or sell gold against dollars upon demand, at this rate. In order to provide more resistance to future inflation, the government should suppress small-denomination paper notes, which would force Americans to once again carry full-weight gold coins in their cash balances.

## 5. The Controversy Concerning the Choice of the New Gold Parity

Within the ranks of those advocating a return of the U.S. to the gold standard, there is controversy over the appropriate exchange rate. The **restorers** want to go back on gold at the rate of $35 per ounce, which was established in the 1934 Gold Reserve Act (and was the gold price used in the Bretton Woods system). The **stabilizers** want to free the market to hold and use gold, then set the dollar to the new price of gold that will be established in the market, even if it happens to be more than $35 per ounce.

The arguments of the restorers are inconsistent. There is nothing "honest" about going back to $35 per ounce. A much stronger case could be made that the pre-1933 price of $20.67 per ounce of gold was the true parity, which Roosevelt then dishonored as one of his first acts in office. Furthermore, the people who were harmed by the prior inflation would not necessarily be the same ones to benefit from a current bout of deflation. For example, it is true that a bond originally issued in (say) 1928, promising to pay $1,000 per year for fifty years, would have had its "real" market value sabotaged when FDR devalued the dollar. Yet if the original purchaser of the bond sold it in (say) 1950, then the new owner has already taken into account the new inflationary regime. The full capital loss has already been absorbed by the original owner. At this point, to raise the purchasing power of the dollar by restoring gold to its former parity, would be to present a gift to the new owner of the bond.

The other major flaw with the restorers' viewpoint is that inflation is harmful not merely because it affects deferred payments. Money is not neutral, and an intentional deflation will have undesirable consequences that will occur in addition to—rather than undoing—the earlier consequences of the inflation.

## Concluding Remarks

The public and most intellectuals lament the consequences of inflation, yet they support those policies (government deficit spending and low interest rates) that require inflation. Only an abandonment of the interventionist mindset, coupled with a return to the classical gold standard, can safeguard the currency.

## *Technical Notes*

- On pages 439–40, Mises laments that even many supporters of sound money do not recognize the danger in bank credit expansion when undertaken to support business (as opposed to financing government deficits). Yet the circulation credit theory of the trade cycle (developed in part III, chapter V) shows the weakness in this thinking. That is why Mises here advocates a complete prohibition on the issuance of new fiduciary media, since he believes it is the only sure way to avoid future crises that will inevitably discredit capitalism. (Note that Mises's suggested reforms would *not* transform the banking system into a 100-percent-reserve arrangement, because the previously issued fiduciary media would still exist.)

- Although they are similar, Mises's proposals (in sections 3 and 4) for currency reform in the generic small country "Ruritania" versus the United States are different. Mises wants to quickly stop the rapidly depreciating currency of Ruritania, the government of which has been **monetizing its deficits**. Mises is content to stop the downward spiral by restoring Ruritania to either a dollar- or a gold-exchange standard. (Recall that the dollar itself was still tied to gold at the official rate of $35 per ounce when Mises wrote these proposals.) For the United States, Mises wants to stop the further issuance of fiduciary media—in order to arrest the boom-bust cycle—and to restore the classical gold standard. This latter objective explains Mises's proposal for abolishing paper notes in denominations of $5,

$10, and perhaps $20, so that the public would carry full-weight gold coins (stamped with $5, $10, etc.) for these transactions.

## *New Terminology*

**Restorers:** Those who want a country to return to a gold standard at a historic parity, a move that would require deflation.

**Stabilizers:** Those who want a country to return to a gold standard by locking in the current market price of gold.

**Monetizing government deficits:** Covering the difference between government expenditures versus tax receipts and loans from private lenders, by resort to the printing press.

## *Study Questions*

1. Explain: "While advocating high prices and wage rates as a panacea and praising the Administration for having raised 'national income' ... to an unprecedented height, they blamed private enterprise for charging outrageous prices and profiteering." (p. 437)

*2. Mises writes (pp. 437–38) that allegedly progressive governments will not abandon their "most formidable weapon, inflation." Yet isn't this a version of the critique of the gold standard (pp. 420–21) that said modern governments were no longer willing to follow the rules of the gold-standard game?

3. In what consists the "eminence of the gold standard"? (p. 438)

4. Why does Mises (humorously) pick the name "John Badman" for the Ruritanian in one of his thought experiments? (p. 446)

5. What is the "incurable defect" of the gold-exchange standard (as opposed to the classical gold standard)? (p. 451)

# APPENDICES

APPENDIX A

# ON THE CLASSIFICATION OF MONETARY THEORIES

*Chapter Outline*

## 1. Catallactic and Acatallactic Monetary Doctrine

Money is such an important part of economic life that writers analyzed it before the development of other areas of economic theory. Even after the development of **catallactics** and the modern subjective theory of value, acatallactic theories of money persist. Yet a necessary condition of a satisfactory theory of money is that it is embedded in a more general theory of exchanges, within which exchanges involving money are merely a component.

Economic theory is difficult, and requires that the economist first consider the formation of prices in the case of direct exchange. Yet eventually the analysis must be generalized to include indirect exchange and the role of money, or else the conclusions may go astray.

## 2. The "State" Theory of Money

The "State" theory of money claims that the value of money rests on the authority of the highest civil power, rather than being the result of valuations in the market. Although its proponents may not realize it, the State theory of money doesn't even attempt to explain the purchasing power of money, which is the primary purpose of a monetary theory.

## 3. Schumpeter's Attempt to Formulate a Catallactic Claim Theory

As an analogy, it is acceptable to call money a claim on the general stock of goods. Yet the notion of money as a claim cannot serve as an actual theory of money, seeking to explain the exchange ratio between money and all other goods and services. Schumpeter has made an attempt to do so, but he was forced at the outset to exclude hoards and other important real-world determinants of the value of money. His failure illustrates that it is a dead end to analyze money as a claim.

## 4. "Metallism"

Knapp defines **metallism** as the monetary doctrine claiming that the unit of value is a certain quantity of metal. Knapp's definition is unclear, but he uses the term to include all those theories of money that are *not* **nominalistic**.

## 5. The Concept "Metallism" in Wieser and Philippovich

Knapp's cumbersome classification scheme has unfortunately been adopted by other economists, allowing the confusion in his work to seep into theirs.

## 6. Note: The Relation of the Controversy about Nominalism to the Problems of the Two English Schools of Banking Theory

Some writers, influenced by Knapp, interpreted the clash between the Currency and Banking Schools as a clash between metallism and nominalism. However, this is not really the crux of their argument. Because he disdained theory altogether, Knapp was unable to even express the actual controversy between the two English schools of thought on banking.

## *Technical Notes*

- In this chapter (e.g., pp. 464 and 473), Mises rejects the theory that the value of money equals the value of the precious metals. This may surprise some readers, since throughout the book Mises clearly endorses the classical gold standard, and he also states that people in commerce (rightly) evaluate coins on their metal content, not on the stamp placed by the legislature. However, there is no contradiction here. Mises agrees that the monetary unit should ultimately be a fixed weight of gold (or another commodity). However, to explain the *value* (or the purchasing power) of that monetary unit, one needs a theory of indirect exchange, grounded in the subjective theory of value.

- In his critique of Schumpeter (in section III), Mises explains that a satisfactory theory of money must take into account all determinants of its purchasing power, including "hoards." For example, if people in the community become fearful and try to accumulate an extra month's worth of expenses in the form of cash, then other things equal the purchasing power of money will rise (i.e., prices will fall). A theory that disregarded the role of hoards would be unable to explain why the value of money changed.

## *New Terminology*

**Catallactics:** The study of exchanges or (more narrowly) the study of monetary exchanges, with an emphasis on the determination of price ratios.

**Metallism:** As defined by Knapp, the monetary doctrine claiming that the unit of value is a certain quantity of metal.

**Nominalism:** The monetary doctrine claiming that the unit of value derives from the government's designation of the legal-tender unit of account.

## Study Questions

1. Explain: "There are problems of theory full comprehension of which can be attained only with the aid of the theory of indirect exchange. To seek a solution of these problems, among which, for example, is the problem of crises, with no instruments but those of the theory of direct exchange, is inevitably to go astray." (p. 462)

2. Explain: "Facts do not speak; they need to be spoken *about* by a theory." (p. 467)

3. Explain: "The State Theory of money—and all acatallactic theories of money in general—breaks down not so much because of the facts, but because it is not able so much as to attempt to explain them." (p. 467)

4. Explain: "In a strict and exact sense . . . all money that is not changing owners at the very moment under consideration is awaiting employment. Nevertheless, it would be incorrect to call such money 'unemployed'; as part of a reserve it satisfies a demand for money, and consequently fulfils the characteristic function of money." (p. 471)

5. Does Mises think that the paper money experiences of the war years pose a refutation of catallactic theories of money? (pp. 480–81)

APPENDIX B

# TRANSLATOR'S NOTE ON THE TRANSLATION OF CERTAIN TECHNICAL TERMS

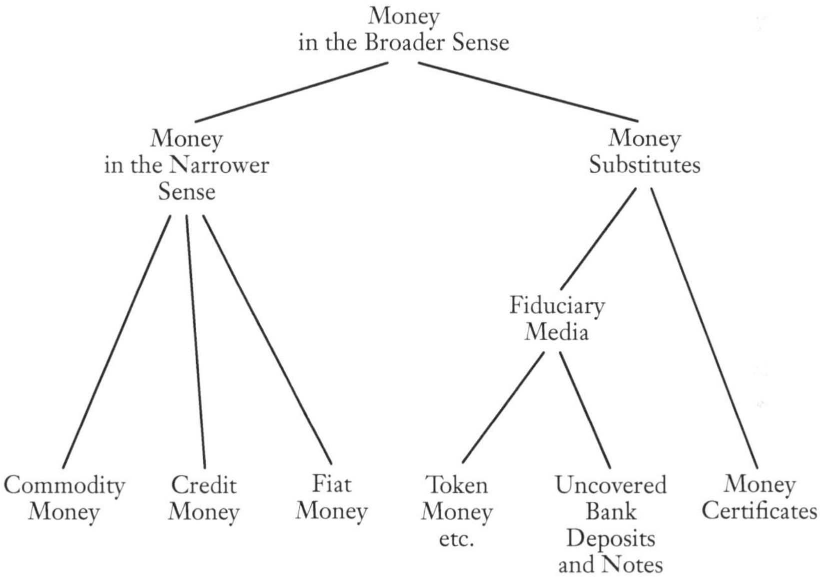


[The translator's note in Appendix B is self-explanatory and needs no summary here. However, we have reproduced the translator's excellent diagram to illustrate the Misesian classification scheme regarding different monetary concepts.]

# GLOSSARY

**Aleatory:** Dependent on chance, luck, or an uncertain outcome.

**Banker:** A person who lends out other people's money.

**Banking School:** An English school of thought which argued that the banks were incapable of independently altering the rate of interest or the purchasing power of money, because the market would use clearing operations, bills of exchange, and other techniques to receive the credit it demanded for business purposes.

**Banknotes:** Paper notes issued by banks, typically entitling the bearer to a specified amount of the money good.

**Bill of exchange:** A non-interest-bearing written order that binds one party to a pay a fixed sum of money to another party at a specified future date or upon demand. A bill of exchange is generally transferable through endorsement.

**Bimetallist legislation:** Efforts by the government to establish a fixed conversion ratio between gold and silver. For example, the government might require that merchants who post a price in gold ounces, also accept payment in silver ounces at a fixed multiple of the gold price.

**Cable rate:** Slang used by foreign-exchange traders to denote the exchange rate between the U.S. dollar and British pound sterling.

**Capital consumption:** A metaphor denoting the reduction in capital because of a failure to reinvest enough out of current output.

**Capitalist:** A person who lends out his or her own money.

**Cash (verb):** To redeem a claim (such as a banknote) by paying the specified amount of the money good.

**Cash flow:** The stream of money payments over time due to an asset or collection of assets.

**Catallactics:** The study of exchanges or (more narrowly) the study of monetary exchanges, with an emphasis on the determination of price ratios.

**Circulation Credit:** A loan granted even though the lender does *not* sacrifice the use of present goods. Circulation credit involves the use of fiduciary media.

**Circulation credit theory of the trade cycle:** The theory developed by Mises (in the present book) explaining the boom phase of the business cycle as due to the artificial expansion of bank credit, made possible by fiduciary media. The bust is then inevitable, as capital goods are malinvested during the boom.

**Classical gold standard:** The system by which a country's currency is redeemable on demand for a fixed weight of gold. In Mises's usage, under a classical gold standard, a portion of the citizens' cash balances consists of actual gold coins and bullion to be used for making purchases.

**Clearing systems:** Arrangements that cancel out or "clear" reciprocal financial claims, so that only net claims need be settled through the actual transfer of money.

**Commodity Credit:** A loan granted through the renunciation of the use of present goods by the lender. Commodity credit may involve money certificates but not fiduciary media.

**Commodity money:** A common medium of exchange that is an economic good in its own right, valued for nonmonetary reasons.

**Convertible Treasury notes:** Paper notes issued by the government that entitle the bearer to redemption in money upon demand.

**Cover (of note issue):** Assets backing the issue of new banknotes. Depending on the regulations, a bank might issue fiduciary media not backed by money itself, but backed by another asset such as a commodity bill.

**Credit:** The ability to receive present goods in exchange for the promise of delivering (typically a greater number of) future goods.

**Credit balance of payments:** The situation occurring when the people of a country collectively spend less on foreign goods and assets than vice versa. It is settled by an inflow of money to the country.

**Credit intermediaries:** Institutions that act as "middlemen" between lenders and borrowers.

**Credit money:** A common medium of exchange that is a claim on a person or legal person (such as a corporation or government agency), not falling due until a (possibly uncertain) future date.

**Currency peg:** The variable and nonlegally-binding rate at which a government is currently maintaining its currency's exchange rate against gold.

**Currency School:** An English school of thought which argued that the banks caused economic crises through the expansion and contraction of credit. However, the Currency School thought the suppression of the issue of fiduciary media in the form of banknotes (which was codified in Peel's Act) would solve the problem, because its members erroneously excluded demand (or current account) deposits from their analysis.

**Current accounts (in banking):** Accounts held with a bank, giving the owner the ability to write drafts or withdraw money upon demand. (Today a standard "checking account" would be an example.)

**Debase:** To dilute the value of the money, for example when a ruler introduces "base" metals into the coinage, reducing their precious-metal content.

**Debit balance of payments:** The situation occurring when the people of a country collectively spend more on foreign goods and assets than vice versa. It is settled by an outflow of money from the country.

**Deflation:** A reduction in the quantity of money that is not offset by a fall in the demand for it, such that prices tend to fall. (Note that this is a technical economic definition, not necessarily having the connotations of "deflation" in popular discussions.)

**Deposit banking:** Banking through the use of circulation credit, where the bank receives deposits into current accounts from one group of clients in order to make loans to another group of borrowers. The depositors consider this money to be part of their cash balances, even though much of it has been lent out to others.

**Devaluation:** The situation in which a country on the flexible standard announces a large drop in the value of its currency against gold.

**Direct exchange:** An exchange in which both parties intend to directly use the received good, either in consumption or production.

**Division of labor:** The situation in which people specialize in particular occupations, producing far more than they personally can consume, and trade away their surplus to receive some of the surplus created by others.

**Equilibrium rate of interest:** The rate of interest corresponding to the true supplies of capital goods and consumer preferences for present versus future consumption. Also known as the natural rate of interest.

**Étatism (as theory):** The doctrine of the omnipotence of the State.

**Étatism (as policy):** The attempt to regulate all social and economic affairs by authoritative commandment and prohibition.

**Exchange rate:** The ratio at which one currency trades against another in the foreign-exchange market.

**Exchange value:** The significance of a good due to its ability to be traded for other goods. (Exchange value can be qualified as either subjective or objective.)

**Fiat money:** A common medium of exchange accepted not because of its technological properties, but because of a special legal designation provided by the appropriate authority. Fiat money is not "backed up" by anything else.

**Fiduciary media:** Money substitutes issued over and above the money (in the narrower sense) held in the redemption fund. Fiduciary media are "unbacked."

**Fixed capital:** Assets embodied in durable investments such as factories and specialized equipment that will be used over a long period.

**Flexible standard:** The system by which a country's currency is redeemable for a variable weight of gold, to be announced by the government at its discretion.

**Foreign-exchange controls:** Government restrictions on the market for foreign currencies.

**Foreign-exchange rate:** The exchange ratio between a domestic and foreign currency.

**Forward contract:** Similar to a futures contract, though a forward contract is not standardized. Furthermore, there is no daily marking-to-market. On the delivery date, the buyer pays the forward price as originally specified in the contract. Thus the forward contract can achieve a positive or negative market value, as conditions change and cause the actual spot price (on the delivery date) to move above or below the originally specified forward price.

**Free banking (among modern Austrians):** The doctrine holding that a free market in banking will pick the optimal fraction of reserves, which may be below 100 percent. Free banking theorists do not believe that the issue of fiduciary media per se causes the business cycle, only that excess quantities of fiduciary media do, and that such an outcome is almost always associated with government-supported issues of fiduciary media.

**Free good:** A good that has a price of zero, because it is not scarce. There is enough of the good to satisfy all human wants that it can technically fulfill.

**Freely-vacillating currency:** A credit or fiat currency that has no official peg to gold at all. Its market price fluctuates just as any commodity.

**Futures contract:** A standardized contract, traded on an organized exchange, where two parties agree to exchange a good at a specified price (the futures price) at a specified future date (the delivery date). As conditions change and alter the futures price pertaining to the delivery date, the exchange will credit or debit the accounts of the buyer and seller of the original futures contract on a daily basis to reflect the change. (If the futures price goes up, the buyer gains and the seller loses, etc.) These daily episodes of marking-to-market restore the market value of the futures contract itself to zero. Upon delivery, the seller of the futures contract delivers the good, while the buyer pays the current spot price for that date, *not* the futures price as originally specified.

**Gold-exchange standard:** The system by which a country's currency is redeemable on demand for a fixed weight of gold, though sometimes only by other governments and central banks. In Mises's usage, under a gold-exchange standard the citizens used only paper notes in everyday transactions, while the actual gold was stored in bank or government vaults.

**Gold standard:** The arrangement by which a nation's money (such as the U.S. dollar or the British pound) can be redeemed for a definite weight of gold.

**Golden rule (of bank lending):** Matching the maturities of assets and liabilities, so that the bank is not dependent on the ability to "roll over" maturing debt. If a bank does not follow the golden rule, increases in short-term interest rates can lead to disaster, when the bank must pay its own creditors while its assets are not yet due.

**Goods of higher orders:** Goods used to produce consumer goods. (A capital good used to produce a consumer good is a second-order good. A capital good used to produce a second-order good is a third-order good, etc.)

**Goods of the first order:** Consumer goods.

**Gresham's Law:** Popularly summarized as "bad money drives out good," the phenomenon by which people will hold money that is undervalued by legislation, and will spend the money that is overvalued by legislation. For example, if bimetallist legislation requires that merchants accept silver and gold at the ratio of 16-to-1, when in fact the actual market exchange rate is 20-to-1, then everyone will try to buy with silver, and no one will use gold for making purchases. Gold will seem to disappear, and only silver will be used in commerce. For a different example, if the government passes legal tender laws on all government-stamped coins, then coins with low metal value (such as U.S. quarters minted in the year 2000) will circulate in trade, whereas coins with high metal content (such as U.S. quarters minted in the year 1950) will be hoarded by people who recognize the value of the silver.

**Hedging transaction:** A financial transaction in which an individual attempts to reduce his or her exposure to a market outcome. For example, someone who believes that Stock XYZ will outperform most other stocks might "go long" by purchasing several thousand shares of it. But to hedge himself against a general fall in the market, he might also "go short" an index fund holding all the stocks in the S&P 500. Thus, even if XYZ falls in price, the investor will still make money, so long as Stock XYZ drops by a smaller amount than most other stocks.

**Hoards (noun):** People who accumulate large cash balances in certain circumstances, allegedly counteracting the predictions of a naïve quantity theory of money.

**Hypothecary loans:** Loans granted with an asset such as real estate serving as collateral.

**Illusive standard:** The system by which a country's currency is pegged to gold at nonmarket rates. The exchange rate is maintained not through the manipulation of gold reserves but rather through the enforcement of foreign-exchange controls.

**Indirect exchange:** An exchange in which at least one party intends to hold the received good, in order to trade it away in the future for something else.

**Inflation:** An increase in the quantity of money (in the broader sense of the term) that is not offset by a corresponding increase in the demand for money (in the broader sense of the term), with the necessary result being a fall in the purchasing power of money. (Note that this is a technical economic definition, not necessarily having the connotations of "inflation" in popular discussions.)

**Inflation tax:** The redistribution of wealth from the citizenry to the government (or its designated beneficiaries) through inflation.

**Inflationism:** Monetary policy that seeks to increase the quantity of money.

**Institutional unemployment:** The situation where workers are qualified and willing to accept jobs at prevailing wage rates, yet cannot find employers to hire them.

**Interest:** Income accruing to the owner of future goods as they mature into present goods, due to the higher valuation placed on present versus future goods.

**Law of diminishing marginal utility:** The rule, deducible from the nature of economizing action, that each additional unit of a good or service will have a lower value, because a person will allocate successive units to satisfying ends that are less and less important.

**Legal tender:** An item that the government declares to be valid for the payment of debts denominated in money, at par value.

**Liquid (adjective):** The ability of being sold for the full market price with a very short search time. (For example, a share of corporate stock is much more liquid than a house.)

**Liquidity:** The situation in which an institution's assets will deliver a cash flow allowing it to pay its liabilities on time. (All liquid enterprises are also solvent, but not necessarily vice versa.)

**Loan banking:** Banking through the use of commodity credit, where the bank receives loans from one group of savers in order to itself make loans to another group of borrowers. The savers do not consider this money as part of their cash balances during the term of the loan to the bank.

**Lower gold point:** Under the gold standard, the minimum market price of gold (quoted in a country's currency) beneath which it is profitable—including all costs of transport, re-coinage, etc.—for citizens to import gold and exchange it with the authorities at the official redemption rate for the domestic currency.

**Market value:** Synonymous with the objective exchange value of a good, typically quoted in money terms.

**Medium of exchange:** A good that is accepted in exchange, with the intention of trading it away to acquire something else in the future.

**Metallism:** As defined by Knapp, the monetary doctrine claiming that the unit of value is a certain quantity of metal.

**Mixed economy:** An economy possessing aspects of both capitalism and socialism, in which private individuals retain nominal ownership of the means of production, but the government extensively regulates their use of this property, including wages, interest rates, and other prices set on the market.

**Monetary policy:** Government or central bank efforts to alter the purchasing power of money.

**Monetizing government deficits:** Covering the difference between government expenditures versus tax receipts and loans from private lenders, by resort to the printing press.

**Money:** A medium of exchange that is generally accepted in the community. Money typically stands on one side of virtually every exchange.

**Money certificates:** Money substitutes that are fully backed by money (in the narrower sense).

**Money cranks:** Very naïve writers who believe that scarcity is an artificial institutional constraint, and that prosperity requires only a sufficient willingness to create more money and/or issue more bank credit.

**Money in the broader sense:** The actual money good (whether commodity, fiat, or credit money), plus money substitutes.

**Money in the narrower sense:** The actual money good (whether commodity, fiat, or credit money), not including money substitutes.

**Money substitute:** A perfectly secure and instantly redeemable claim on money, which itself circulates as money (in the broader sense) because it fulfills the functions of money.

**Money rate of interest:** The rate of interest determined in the marketplace for loans of money. (The money rate can deviate from the equilibrium [or natural] rate of interest, in a process that is explained in part III of the book.)

**Naïve inflationism:** Inflationism supported by the belief that money constitutes wealth.

**Nominalism:** The monetary doctrine claiming that the unit of value derives from the government's designation of the legal-tender unit of account.

**Objective exchange value of money:** The possibility of obtaining a certain quantity of other goods in exchange for a unit of money.

**Objective theory of value:** An explanation of value that relies on the objective properties of a good, such as its cost of production or the amount of labor that went into its construction. (The classical economists, such as Adam Smith and David Ricardo, held an objective theory of value.)

**Paper standard:** The arrangement by which the government does not redeem paper notes for a precious metal. (A paper standard stands in contrast to a gold standard.)

**Parallel Standard:** A monetary system in which two different goods both serve as monies. (For example, gold and silver might both serve as money under a Parallel Standard.)

**Peel's Act [Bank Charter Act 1844]:** An important legislative act that took the power of issuing new notes away from private banks and vested it completely with the Bank of England, which itself was required to maintain 100 percent metallic backing for any new notes that it issued. However, the Act crucially did *not* impose such a restriction on the extension of deposits, meaning that private banks could create more fiduciary media by granting loans (not backed by gold) to their customers.

**Price controls:** Government decrees threatening fines or other punishment for people trading at prices that are either too high (in the case of a price ceiling) or too low (in the case of a price floor).

**Price of money:** The quantity of goods (or services) that must be given up in exchange to acquire a unit of money.

**Prices:** The market exchange ratios between various goods and services. In a monetary economy, prices are typically quoted in terms of the money good.

**Private capital:** The aggregate of the products that serve as a means to the acquisition of goods.

**Purchasing power:** The amount of goods and services that a unit of money can command because of the various prices in the market.

**Purchasing power/inflation premium:** An increase in the contractual rate of interest due to the expected rise in prices.

**Purchasing Power Parity:** The theory stating that the exchange ratio between two monies is determined by the respective exchange ratios of each money and other goods and services.

**Quantity theory of money:** An old doctrine explaining changes in the purchasing power of money by reference to the quantity of money and the demand to hold it. (There are many versions of the quantity theory, with the more mechanical ones—which posit that a doubling of the money stock will lead to a doubling of all prices—being obviously wrong.)

**Real wages:** Wage rates relative to the prices of goods and services.

**Regression Theorem:** Mises's argument that the current purchasing power of money is influenced by people's memory of yesterday's purchasing power. The causality is traced back in time, until the point at which the money good was valued as a regular commodity in direct exchange.

**Restorers:** Those who want a country to return to a gold standard at a historic parity, a move that would require deflation.

**Restrictionism/Deflationism:** Monetary policy that aims at raising the objective exchange value of money.

**Scale of values:** An analytical tool by which the economist interprets the actions of an individual, who subjectively ranks particular units of goods and services in order from most to least important.

**Seigniorage:** The difference between the market value of money and the cost to produce it.

**Shortages:** A shortfall in the quantity of goods offered for sale, compared to the amount consumers wish to purchase. Shortages are caused when a price ceiling holds the price below the market-clearing level.

**Social (productive) capital:** The aggregate of the products intended for employment in further production.

**Solvency:** The situation in which the market value of an institution's assets exceeds its liabilities.

**Stabilizers:** Those who want a country to return to a gold standard by locking in the current market price of gold.

**Subjective theory of value:** An explanation of value that relies on individuals' subjective rankings of particular units of goods and services. (The so-called Marginal Revolution of the early 1870s—spearheaded by Carl Menger, William Stanley Jevons, and Léon Walras—overturned the objective theory of value and ushered in the subjective theory.)

**Subsistence fund:** A concept used by Böhm-Bawerk to denote the savings the capitalists must have first accumulated, in order to feed and otherwise support the workers as they engage in time-consuming production processes.

**Token coins:** Coins that serve as representatives of money (usually in very small denominations), even though they do not contain the full weight of metal in the case of a commodity money.

**Upper gold point:** Under the gold standard, the maximum market price of gold (quoted in a country's currency) above which it is profitable—including all costs of transport, re-coinage, etc.—for foreigners to exchange the domestic currency for gold (at the official redemption rate, which is below the current market price), and have the gold shipped out of the original country.

**Use-value:** The significance of a good due to its ability to be directly used by the owner in consumption or production. (Use-value can be qualified as either subjective or objective.)

**Value:** The importance that an individual places on a particular unit of a good or service.

**(Wicksellian) natural rate of interest:** Developed by economist Knut Wicksell, the hypothetical rate of interest that would occur if goods were traded directly against each other without the use of money.

**Working capital:** Current assets minus current liabilities. More generally, a measure of a firm's ability to quickly turn some of its assets into cash in order to finance an expansion.

# INDEX

## J



## L



## M



## P



## Q